Contents

Foreword by Dave Turton 8th Dan; Officially the high
in the U.K. and Founder / Head of the Self Defence Fe

CW00889149

Foreword

Having been involved in the 'self-defence & self-protection' fields since 1964 and having achieved a certain 'level' of expertise over these decades, I have come across dozens of books supposedly informing the readers of how best to make their lives safer and less fearful of violent encounters.

These books range from, more or less, dangerously useless to occasionally genuine and valid. The latter sadly are in the minority.

So, when Alan Bell, the Representative for the SDF in his region of Scotland and a very decent, intelligent guy to boot asked me to review and comment on this book, I have to admit I was a bit worried. After all, just being a nice guy and an SDF Representative doesn't mean I could just write glowing tributes to his written work.

Also, frankly I am not keen on voicing my opinion on something as obviously close to someone's heart for fear of offending him or her.

Thankfully any reticence I felt was dispelled very quickly once I started reading the material.

Every so often, in with the rubbish, you come across a nugget of gold. This book happily ranks as 22 carat.

Any book has to fill certain criteria, more so when the book is aimed at 'sensible advice';

Firstly, it has to do what the book title implies. Often I read so-called self-defence or personal safety books to find that the contents bare little resemblance to the title.

Secondly, the book has to have the right 'presentation' i.e. a decent cover, well set out contents and, where necessary, clear and concise illustrations or photos.

Thirdly, it has to 'read well'. This is not always the case as some really talented 'experts' can't get their points across lucidly.

Finally, the Author has to be a credible writer of the actual subject he or she is writing about.

In Alan's case, he meets all four criteria easily. His credentials are impeccable; His experience long and genuine (he is NO 'Walter Mitty' type); His knowledge of the subjects he is covering is vast; His teaching experience is long and varied.

So thankfully I have come across another 'gold nugget' and consequently so have you, the Reader.

Alan's book IS a *complete* book of personal safety. It isn't a 'mish-mash' of martial arts type techniques, often unworkable in real situations. He understands the necessity of trying to AVOID confrontations rather than simply giving a few techniques gleaned from the martial arts.

So, if you are looking for a book of 'high flying oriental flashy methods', look elsewhere. If however you are looking for realistic, reasonable, workable advice and methods, look no further.

Alan's advice is sensible and correct and following this advice WILL make you safer. The illustrations are clear, as are the explanations. The 'target' readers are anyone rather than just fit young men and women looking for more martial arts methods. The contents are well thought out and easily followed by all.

If you are thinking of buying a book that frankly will make your chances of living in an increasingly violent society that much safer and you only wish to purchase ONE good one rather than a plethora of 'so-so' books, then you have found it.

I often struggle to recommend books when asked; Alan has made that struggle redundant. I heartily recommend this work to anyone interested in their own personal safety and that of their loved ones.

David Turton 8th Dan: Head of the Self-Defence Federation U.K.

1. Introduction to the Author

For many years now, the martial arts have been touted as a great forum for learning personal safety skills, in particular, self defence – and while, in a few cases this may be true, generally it most definitely is not.

Most martial arts are dojo / classroom based, awash with rules and regulations. They invariably teach rehearsed moves and techniques which, if taken into a street fight scenario, just would not work. Techniques such as using your forearm to block a kick (for example, a Shito Ryu in Karate) or squeezing your attacker's hand down against your head to release a hair pull (used in various martial arts including Tae Kwon Do) or how to get out of a bear hug.

Yes, they look great in a dojo where your attacker is conditioned to respond to your counter attack and they cannot deviate from their set moves for fear of breaching a rule or regulation but in reality you are likely to break your forearm if you try to block a full force kick and your attacker would not just grab your hair in a hair pull – he would grab your hair and drag you to the ground, leaving your hand squeeze ineffectual.

And when is the last time you saw a bear hug used in a real-life street fight? More likely, your attack from behind will be a strangle hold takedown or a strike to the back of the head – but a bear hug? Come on!!

So why do so many martial arts teach ineffectual techniques? Well, you have to remember that all martial arts are exactly what they say they are – an artistic way of performing martial or warlike moves. Martial arts have been performed and passed down through generations and they have their own customs and traditions. That is not to say that all martial arts are rubbish. They all have their place – in increasing speed, agility, strength, stamina, confidence and discipline.

But whereas martial arts may have been effective when first developed hundreds of years ago against invaders and ancient weapons, many have now become ineffective – at least in some of their moves and/or techniques. They have become outdated, toned down and, in some cases, theatrical.

It is time to move into the 21st Century.

Some martial arts are realising this and adapting, but others are still stuck in traditionalism.

Since 1997, Alan Bell has been teaching modern self defence and personal safety skills, the principle being that if someone wants to learn how to defend themselves, they don't want to have to devote themselves to years of training to gain a black belt and become proficient in self defence. Most people want to learn how to defend themselves now, today, learning simple but effective techniques. And if they enjoy learning these skills, perhaps they will join a martial arts club and hone up on what they have learned.

Rather than a 'martial art', Alan sees his modern self defence teaching as 'the art of fighting' and takes his fighting style from the instruction he received both in the military and in the close protection (bodyguard) industry.

He began learning martial arts back in 1979 when he first entered a Judo dojo. He then took up Karate before moving on to Kick Boxing, Ju-jitsu and Western Boxing. But it was during his military career that he learned the real meaning of 'defensive fighting'.

Having spent 6 years with the British Army's Royal Military Police – originally with a Reservist unit before moving onto a Specialist unit and latterly transferring to the Special Air Service, Alan was unfortunately medically discharged after suffering a knee injury but he quickly realised that there was an enormous gap between modern unarmed combat training using realistic scenarios and traditional martial arts.

The author is on the left of this photo during a STAR (Search Tactics And Rescue) exercise **The author in full 'black kit' minus anti-flash lens on his respirator.**

After his military career, Alan moved into the world of Close Protection and became a bodyguard for business executives, celebrities and members of Royalty. It was at this time that he became involved with 'The National Federation for Personal Safety', becoming an instructor and teaching with police officers in Scotland's Strathclyde Police and Northern Constabulary and with officers from the Metropolitan Police in London.

As the new millennium evolved, Alan began to open his instruction up to the public instead of just police forces and he was also accepted by Dave Turton's 'Self Defence Federation (UK)', initially as an instructor, and latterly as both instructor and Regional Representative for the SDF (UK) in the Highlands & Islands of Scotland.

In 2007, Alan was approached by the 'International Combatives Self Defense Association', a newly formed organisation based in the USA which is dedicated to military & civilian combatives, personal safety and law enforcement defensive tactics. Having heard of Alan's background and his realistic, quality driven programmes, the Director of the ICSDA offered Alan the role of Scottish Director and this was swiftly enhanced to include the role of 'Close Quarter Combat' Admissions Director for the whole of the ICSDA.

In 2008, Alan was offered the position of 'European Director' of the 'International Combatives Self Defence Association'.

As with most modern self defence instructors, Alan uses these professional contacts to continually improve himself, adapting new defensive systems and techniques to improvise and hone his skills.

Alan's reputation as an innovative, realistic, self defence instructor has also grown and, as well as having taught individuals from many worldwide police and military units including Greek Special Forces, US Special Forces, German Special Forces and British Royal Protection Squads, he regularly instructs members of the public including martial artists, doormen, prison and police officers. Also, alongside officers from various UK police forces, he teaches school pupils, students, victims of attack and businesses.

He has appeared on numerous television programmes, most notably ITV's "Tonight with Sir Trevor MacDonald" and he has written articles for an array of magazines, newspapers and newsletters on a variety of personal safety and self defence topics including Personal Safety for Women, Street Self Defence, Anti-Carjack Techniques, Evasive & Defensive Driving Skills, Personal Safety for Students, Self Defence during Pregnancy, Attack Proofing your Children and Personal Safety in the Workplace.

So, how is Alan's training different from most traditional martial arts? Well, it is entirely based on real-life scenarios. There are 'martial arts' and there are 'fighting skills' and Alan's training falls firmly into the latter category. Real-life attackers use fists, kicks, knees, head butts, bites and weapons including broken bottles, baseball bats and knives. 'Attackers' in Alan's classes will not say when or what part of the body they will attack and will invariably be shouting abuse and acting in a threatening manner. Sometimes a defender can talk them down and de-escalate the situation – sometimes they can't.

This, combined with instruction on the 'Use of Reasonable Force' and the 'Law regarding Self Defence' as well as the ramifications of using force in a self defence situation, forms the basis of Alan's personal safety / self defence instruction.

Compared with traditional martial arts training – they really are poles apart.

For example, in 2004, Alan was instructing a female who had attained a black belt in Karate. So why was she taking part in his self defence class? It was because a few months previous she had been attacked from behind by a lone assailant and raped.

This young lady could not understand how she, a martial art's black belt, could have been defeated by an attacker, far less raped. Prior to the attack, she was confident that her martial arts skills could fend off any attack – but her training could not protect her.

Unlike a martial arts combatant, a real-life attacker will not rely on an adjudicator to say when to start and stop an attack, will not play by any rules and, in most cases, will not be concerned if you live or die.

So make sure that when you are training, that you are training for today's world. 'Train hard, fight easy' is a creed used in certain units of the British military - never has it been so true as in today's society, where our streets are, on the odd occasion, quite literally, a battle ground.

The author 'padded up' for a *Security And Safety* self defence lesson

Are you ready?

For further information on Security And Safety and their personal safety / self defence systems, visit **www.securityandsafety.co.uk** or send us an email to **enquiries@ www. securityandsafety.co.uk**

"All that is necessary for the triumph of evil is that good men do nothing."
Edmund Burke, 1770

2. Personal Awareness

Unfortunately, we live in an increasingly violent society in which, although in some areas of the world, crime is low, the fear of crime is always high. Here are some statistics taken from UK records:

- 1 in 3 students will become victims of crime during their first year at university or college and 1 in 4 students will have their accommodation broken into.[1]
- 33% of teenagers experience some form of domestic abuse at home.[2]
- 6% UK of teenage girls have been forced to have sex by their boyfriends and think it is acceptable.[3]
- 1 in 5 young men & 1 in 10 young women think violence against women is acceptable.[4]
- 1 in 5 workers are subject to violent attacks at work.[5]
- 1 in 4 teachers are subject to violent attacks by pupils.[6]
- Almost 1 in 3 nurses are subjected to physical assaults or verbal abuse at least *once a month*.[7]
- Someone is attacked by a complete stranger in Britain every 30 seconds. (A survey released in 2009, showed that there were 1,057,000 violent attacks by strangers - the equivalent of 2,895 a day or 120 every hour).[8]
- *Every minute* in the UK, the police receive a call from the public for assistance for domestic violence [9]but only 40.2% of domestic violence is reported.[10]
- *Every 20 seconds* a woman is hit by her partner.[11]
- Men in Scotland are *more than twice* as likely of being murdered as those in England & Wales and almost twice as likely to commit murder or kill themselves as people anywhere else in Britain.[12]
- European women aged 16 – 44 are more likely to be injured or die from domestic violence than from road accidents & cancer *combined*.[13]
- 1 woman dies *every 3 days* due to injuries received from abusive partners.[14]

2.1 Personal Awareness; Your first line of defence

Most people think of knees to the groin and Bruce Lee type moves when they hear the term 'self defence'. However, true self defence begins long before any actual physical contact starts. The first, and probably the most important, part of self defence is personal awareness; Awareness of yourself, your surroundings, and any potential threat or danger.

Remember, an attacker almost always adopts the element of surprise to their advantage. Studies have shown that attackers will choose targets who appear to be unaware of their surroundings and what is going on around them – cash points are perfect examples.

---

[1] Home Office Development & Practice Report 21: Crimes Against Students; Emerging Lessons for Reducing Student victimisation, March 2004
[2] NSPCC & Sugar survey, March 2005
[3] NSPCC & Sugar survey, March 2005
[4] NSPCC & Sugar survey, March 2005
[5] Trade Union Congress, 1999
[6] Association of Teachers and Lecturers, 2009
[7] European NEXT Study, Violence Risks in Nursing, March 2008
[8] British Crime Survey, 2008
[9] Stanko, 2000
[10] Dodd et al, July 2004
[11] Home Office, Crime in England & Wales 2006/7 report
[12] Scottish Government: Lessons for Mental Health Care in Scotland, 2008
[13] Ramonet I. Violence Begins at Home, Le monde Diplomatique (English edition) July 2004
[14] Dodd et al, July 2004

By being alert, confident and aware of your surroundings most confrontations can be avoided.

How can you avoid this trap?

It is easier to tell you about the different conditions of awareness first:

2.2 Awareness Conditions

Condition White: *Unaware.*
A complete lack of awareness. 'Switched off' is where 95% of people are, 95% of their time. These people describe an attack as happening "suddenly".

Condition Yellow: *Aware*.
Permanently 'switched on' or 'on guard'. Aware of your surroundings and any inherent dangers.

Condition Orange: *Alert.*
This condition is triggered by a hint of threat or danger or if something looks suspicious.

Condition Red: *Reacting.*
Fight or flight.

The above colour coded awareness conditions were developed by Lieutenant Colonel Jeff Cooper back in the 1960's and is still used by military and law enforcement bodies throughout the World today. So how does it work?

Well, let's take you back to that cash point example again; you are walking towards the cash point listening to your iPod and texting your mate on your mobile phone. You get to the cash point, stick your card in and withdraw £50. As you go to take your cash out you are suddenly pushed out of the way by a tall, skinny dude with a hoodie top who grabs your cash and your card before sprinting off down the street.

This is a form of 'mugging' that many criminals make a good living from. But how did it happen?

The answer is simple – because you were unaware of your surroundings.

No doubt your statement to the police following this incident would begin "Suddenly this guy came out of no-where …" but nothing happens "suddenly" in life. There are always clues or signs that something is about to occur.

Now, let's try that same scenario again only adopting the colour coded system of awareness;

You are walking towards the cash point listening to your iPod and texting your mate on your mobile phone - **Condition White** (Although this is a no-no straight away, I will give you the benefit of the doubt and assume that, on this one occasion, you were listening to your iPod when you received and replied to a text message. That said, ideally you should be in Condition Yellow all of the time).

You glance up as you make your approach to the cash point and notice a tall, skinny dude with a hoodie top eyeing you up (Figure A) – **Condition Yellow**.

Figure A

Figure B

As you get to the cash point you notice the tall, skinny dude with a hoodie top casually edging his way towards you (Figure B) – **Condition Orange**.

Now, you have two choices – leave the cash point for another time (the safest option) or carry on.

Let's say you carry on. You stick your card in and withdraw £50. As you go to take your cash out you see the tall, skinny dude with a hoodie top lunge towards you (Figure C) – **Condition Red**.

Figure C

Now, because you were aware of your surroundings, you can react more positively. You could turn to face him, blocking the cash point at the same time and bring your hands up to adopt a defensive stance.

If the tall, skinny dude with the hoodie top still tries to take your cash, you can defend yourself either with your hands and feet or by using your debit card as a slashing improvised weapon. Either way, the attacker is effectively dealt with and won't be getting your cash.

Have a look at this sentence. Read it through once, then again and register in your mind how many "F"s there are in the sentence. Don't cheat by reading the answer first. Just count the "F"s.

Finished files are the result of years of scientific study combined with the experience of years.

Some people will read this sentence and see three F's, some see four or five but, in fact, there are six F's. Sometimes our brains see things but just don't take them in. What has this got to do with personal safety?

2.3 Warning Signs & Danger Signs
Every human being, and quite a few animals, will display *Warning Signs* and *Danger Signs* before they attack.

Warning Signs

- Direct, prolonged eye contact.
- Breathing accelerates.
- Facial colour darkens (flushing).
- Stands tall to maximise height.
- Head is back.
- Kicking the ground.
- Large movements with hands in particular.

Danger Signs

- Clenching and unclenching of fists.
- Facial colour pales.
- Lips tighten over teeth.
- Head drops forward to protect the throat.
- Eyebrows drop to protect the eyes.
- Hands rise above the waist, shoulders tense.
- Aggressor looks at body target.
- Stance changes to sideward to protect the vital organs.

Figure A: Warning Signs   **Figure B: Danger Signs**

The perfect example for witnessing all of these signs simultaneously is the drunken brawl where, in an inebriated state, we lose our civilized inhibitions and revert back to the basic instincts in us and every animal.

Warning Signs are displayed as the drunk shouts and gestures wildly, throws his arms wide and pushes his chin up to make himself look taller and wider (Figure A). Exactly the same behaviour can be seen as a grizzly bear stands up to display its size before an attack or a peacock showing off its tail feathers whilst strutting and kicking the ground before an attack, etc.

At this stage, take your cue and leave because the Danger Signs then signify that the person is about to strike (Figure B). All you can do at this stage is get ready to defend yourself because it is too late to escape.

The transition from Warning Sign to Danger Sign can be seconds and not all of the signs may be shown, for example, you may spot someone staring at you from across the room. You can tell by his eyes that this is not a case of 'do I know you?' or amorous intent. As this person begins to approach you, their eyebrows drop and they clench their fists.

Once you realise that everyone displays these Warning and Danger Signs before they attack, it becomes easier to prevent or avoid it.

Sixth Sense – Use it.

Deja-vous, sixth sense, instincts, intuition (especially if you are a woman); whatever you want to call it, your subconscious will invariably help you 'feel' good or bad about a situation or a person. This may even be us subconsciously picking up on the other person's Warning and Danger Signs.

All of us, but especially women, have this intuitive feeling but very few of us pay attention to it.

Learn to trust your intuition and use it to your full advantage. If a person or a situation makes you feel unsafe or uncomfortable - get away from it. Your intuition may be trying to tell you something, so listen to it.

Example:

You are walking home late at night. It's dark and the streets are deserted but at the end of this particular street is a bus stop and you know you can catch a bus there in about twenty minutes time. You begin to hear footsteps behind you and upon glancing back see a man coming towards you, his pace quickening. What do you do?

You should first of all cross the road. Hopefully the man was just trying to get to the bus stop and he will now pass you by on the opposite side of the street.

But what if he crosses the road too? Now you still do not know if this was a coincidence. Did he want to look in a particular shop window? Does he live on this side of the street? To be sure, you cross back again, hopefully leaving him once again on the opposite side of the street.

But this time, he too crosses back over the street. You have definitely confirmed that the man is after you and not the bus – but you still don't know why. He could want to ask you if you know when the next bus is. He may want to know the time because he knows what time the next bus is due. He may ask for a light for his cigarette.

Now what do you do? Well, you could run – but you may not be wearing appropriate footwear (high heels, shoes with little grip, etc.) and a person who runs often excites an attacker as it shows they are afraid, so he has already won the fight psychologically.

I have read magazines where so-called experts have said "Hide under the nearest vehicle" but again, you still have not found out what this man wants and how can you defend yourself from under a vehicle?

The best thing to do is to turn around and face the man. What does this achieve?

Firstly, you can now see the man. You can remember his facial features, his clothing, his height – in other words, you can describe him to the police if you need to and you can recognise him if you should ever see him again.

Secondly, if this man was intent on attacking you, he would have much preferred to do so from behind. Now he will have to think twice before committing himself to an attack where he can possibly be identified.

Thirdly, you can now defend yourself if need be. It is practically impossible to defend yourself with your back to an attacker, this way you are ready for anything.

At this stage, having confirmed that he is stalking you and having turned around to face him, you could ask the man what he wants. A simple "Can I help you?" will do in case he does want to know the time. But I would suggest following this up with "Don't I know you from somewhere?" or "Oh, it's you. Now where have I seen your face before?"

This will throw any prospective attacker right off. Just think what is going through his mind now; "Damn, she has turned around to face me. I've got to be careful she doesn't get a good look at me." Closely followed by; "Damn, now she thinks she recognises me. How long will it be before she remembers I work at the local supermarket?"

Do you think he would carry out an attack now – or move along to more 'unaware' victim?

Remember at this stage that he could be innocent enough. He may ask you for the correct time or a light or directions – but these are also ploys used by attackers to put you off guard, so be aware and simply say "No" to every question;

- Do you have the time? "NO".
- Do you know when the next bus is due? "NO".
- Do you have a light? "NO".
- Do you know where High Street is? "NO".

All the time, adopt a pose which can quickly become defensive for example, hand resting thoughtfully on chin the other folded across your body. Legs shoulder width apart, knees slightly bent (see Figure A).

Figure A

Figure B

If this man decides to carry on and attack you, you will be ready to react, you will be able to identify him and you will be in a much better position to defend yourself (See Figure B).

3. The Right to Defend Yourself

Unfortunately, no matter how much we practice personal awareness and violence avoidance techniques, there may come a time when we find ourselves in a physical confrontation. Whether or not you have self defence training and no matter what your age or physical condition, it is important to understand that you can and should defend yourself physically. You have both a moral and a legal right to do so.

Many people are afraid to defend themselves when attacked in case they are taken to court, imprisoned for assault or simply make matters worse. Assault statistics however clearly show that your odds of survival are far greater if you do fight back.

So, when can you defend yourself?

3.1 The Law

Well the Law will tell you and although each country has their own version of law, most revolve around the same basic principle of the right of self defence. As Great Britain set about conquering the world in past history, so their law went with them – with the Pilgrim Fathers to the USA, Scots being forced to leave their Highland homes and settle in the USA, Canada, Australia and New Zealand, the Commonwealth states in India, Africa and the Caribbean, English penal colonies in Australia, even the crusaders as they marched through Europe and into the Middle East.

With that in mind, I have chosen English Law as an illustrative example of the 'Right to Defend Yourself'.

CRIMINAL LAW REGARDING USE OF FORCE

Section 3 (1) of the Criminal Law Act 1967 states:
"A person may use such force as is reasonable in the circumstances in the prevention of a crime, or in effecting or assisting in the lawful arrest of offenders or suspected persons unlawfully at large."

In layman's terms, what exactly does this mean? Well, you are allowed to use such force as is **reasonably necessary** to:

- Defend yourself,
- Defend others,
- Protect your property, and to
- Make a citizen's arrest.

3.2 The Use of Reasonable Force

Seems straightforward enough – you are allowed to use such force as is reasonably necessary to defend yourself - but then doesn't that mean that you have to think about the amount of force you will use to defend yourself? How much force are you legally allowed to use and how much would be deemed excessive?

The interpretation of "**Reasonable Force**" used depends upon;

- The gravity of the crime being prevented.
- Whether it was possible to prevent it by non-violent means.
- Whether you were willing to try those means first.
- The relative strength of the parties involved.

Let's analyse these points one at a time;

The gravity of the crime being prevented

If someone grabs your wrist and won't let you go, the amount of force you use to stop them or get away would be minimal – perhaps a breakaway technique or the use of a pressure point.

If someone grabs your throat with the apparent intent on strangling you, the amount of force you use to stop this will also increase – and as your attacker's intent is lethal, you are allowed to match this intent to get away or stop the attack. In other words, you can kill your attacker (although, obviously, this would not be your intention). A blow to the throat will definitely shift him off you and this may not have a lasting effect on him – or it may kill him. In either case, you will be legally within your rights to do so as his intent was lethal.

So, as the gravity of the crime or seriousness of the attack increases, from a grab to a strike to a strangle hold or whatever, so the level of your response can also increase, from a breakaway technique to a strike to using an improvised weapon.

Whether it was possible to prevent it by non-violent means

Now, before you are allowed to use any force to defend yourself, you must first see if there is any way of preventing it. This could simply be shouting at your attacker as he approaches you. A loud, aggressive "Get back" may be enough to warn your attacker off, particularly if he is looking for an easy target.

It also means looking for an escape route. If your attacker is coming towards you and there is an exit behind you, then taking that exit would prevent the attack from occurring. Likewise, crossing the road or raising your hands in a defensive pose before striking (assuming you had the time and distance) would all be deemed as non-violent ways to stop an attacker.

Whether you were willing to try those means first

Easy enough! If you could have simply used an escape route to walk away from an attack or shouted at your attacker to "Stop", did you actually try these means before you defended yourself?

The relative strength of the parties involved

The amount of force you used to stop a little old lady would be far less than the force you would use to stop a 300lb power lifter. It may be deemed that simply pinning the old lady's arms to her side would be a reasonable use of force whereas, in the case of the power lifter, you may be allowed to punch, kick or even use an improvised weapon.

So, you now know the exact wording of the Law, when you can defend yourself and the amount of force you can use to stop an attacker that would be deemed "reasonable". But is your right to defend yourself crystal clear in your mind?

Example:

You are in a bar. There is only one way in and one way out. The bar is too narrow to move about much and there are hardly any other people in the bar. A drunk walks in and looking right at you shouts "I'm gonna knock your head off." With clenched fists he approaches you and punches you on the jaw. "There's more where that came from" he shouts, pointing his finger at you threateningly, he walks away. Can you chase after him and defend yourself?

Well, if you did, you may be able to argue that you were making a citizen's arrest but it is likely that the Courts will deem your actions to be an assault. It cannot be self defence because the drunk was walking away from you so you have nothing to defend yourself against.

A judge will usually ask "Did you feel threatened?" and if you can prove that you did, you have the right to defend yourself. If you cannot prove this or the judge does not think that you could have felt threatened, then it is not self defence.

Let's change this scenario slightly. Same bar, same drunk. He still shouts "I'm gonna knock your head off", with clenched fists he approaches you and punches you on the jaw. But this time, as he shouts "There's more where that came from", he raises his hand to strike you again. Now can you defend yourself?

"Did you feel threatened?" – Yes, you can defend yourself now.

So, in the eyes of the Law, you need to wait until your attacker strikes you before you can defend yourself, right?

Wrong!

You are allowed to defend yourself if you feel threatened and there is no other means of escape and you tried to prevent the attack by non-violent means before you defended yourself.

So, the question is "When did you feel threatened?"

Same scenario, same drunk. He enters the bar, you spot the warning signs as he stares at you, his face is flushed, and he verbally tells you in an aggressive manner "I'm gonna knock your head off". His hands now form fists – danger sign. As he approaches, realizing there is no other exit, you raise your arms in a defensive pose and shout "Get back" at the top of your voice. He still comes at you ……. And you were forced to defend yourself.

You struck first. He has not touched you yet, but his intention to strike made you feel threatened and, after trying to stop him by non-violent means failed, you were forced to strike him and stop the attack.

That's self defence!

Hopefully this example has helped clarify when you can and cannot defend yourself and, by association, when you can and cannot defend others. Take a look at the Reasonable Force Quiz (Appendix A) to test your understanding further.

3.3 Protecting Your Property

I mentioned before that you are allowed to use reasonable force to defend your property however this is a contentious reason to use force because it is often misunderstood and, unlike the right to defend yourself, it is not always allowed in every country so please check out the country or state you live in before assuming you have the right to defend your property.

In the UK, people have often thought 'your home is your castle' to coin a phrase. If anyone entered your property or tried to enter your property, you had the right to use force to stop them. This however is a somewhat grey area which I hope to clear up for you by using an actual case study.

Late one night in August 1999, Tony Martin was alone in the upstairs bedroom of his farm house in a remote village in Norfolk, England, when he heard a crash downstairs.

Two burglars, Fred Barras and Brendan Fearon, had entered the ground floor of Mr. Martin's property so, being a farmer, Mr. Martin picked up his shotgun and headed downstairs to confront them.

Later in Court, Mr. Martin would say "I heard this murmuring and had this light shone in my eyes. All these things happened in a flash. I couldn't stand it any longer and then I just let the gun off. When you resort to using a gun, you are desperate. I've never used that shotgun before. I'm not really interested in shooting rabbits round the house. I didn't even know if it worked. I discharged the gun and then ran upstairs. Nobody followed me."

Fred Barras was killed after being shot in the back. Brendon Fearon was shot in the leg and groin.

Both men had a string of convictions between them and had travelled from Newark, Nottinghamshire, to burgle Mr. Martin's home.

From the outset Mr. Martin claimed that he shot at Fearon and Barras in self defence. He also claimed that his home had been plagued by burglars for years and as nothing had been done to prevent this re-occurring, he had lost faith in the police.

At the court case, a number of important points were brought to light;

The Winchester pump-action shotgun which Mr. Martin used to 'defend' himself was not legally owned by him. Mr. Martin claimed he 'found' the weapon.

Doubt was raised as to where exactly Mr. Martin was when he fired at the two burglars. He initially said that he was in his bedroom when he was woken by the noise of the break-in. He said he picked up his shotgun and made his way downstairs and on his way down, a torch was shone in his eyes and he fired.

The Court heard a different version of events from the Prosecution as they maintained that Mr. Martin was lying in wait for the burglars in the darkness of the ground floor of his home. They claimed Fred Barras was not only murdered but effectively "executed" by Mr. Martin and they backed up their claims with forensic evidence which concluded that at least two of the shots must have been fired by Mr. Martin while he was downstairs.

Mr. Martin's defence took the "tactical" decision of agreeing that all the shots had been fired downstairs. This tactic would enable them to argue 'self defence' as opposed to going along with Mr. Martin's original statement that he had fired once from the stairs then pursued the burglars downstairs. If this did occur, it would be difficult to prove he 'felt threatened' and, as the burglars were retreating, it would be very difficult to paint the picture of a terrified Mr. Martin trying to defend himself.

Doubt was also raised into Mr. Martin's mental state as the Prosecution depicted him as an angry man, revealing that he had once talked of "putting gypsies in one of his fields surrounded by barbed wire and machine gunning them". This statement was highlighted because both Fearon and Barras came from a travelling community (commonly referred to as gypsies).

In the end, the jury clearly believed he fired in anger and convicted Mr. Martin for the murder of Fred Barras.

Following an appeal, his murder conviction and life jail sentence were downgraded to manslaughter and five years imprisonment respectively.

In February 2003, Brendon Fearon, who had at the time more than 30 convictions to his name, was jailed for supplying heroin outside a police station. He was hoping to win up to £100,000 in damages from Tony Martin for the injuries received which he said had stopped him from working, affected his sex life and ruined his hobby of martial arts. He also claimed he was suffering from post-traumatic stress disorder and was too frightened to watch fireworks or gunfights on television. He was constantly seen walking with a limp and a walking stick until a national newspaper photographed him cycling a bike and climbing stairs unaided.

There was further public outcry when it emerged that Mr. Fearon had received legal aid to sue Mr. Martin while Mr. Martin had to fund his own defence.

In August 2003, Tony Martin was released from prison after serving two-thirds of his five-year sentence.

So, when can we defend our property and with what force?

Let me highlight this Law by giving another example:

You are in bed when you hear a noise downstairs. You get up and grab the golf club you keep at the side of your bed in case anyone ever breaks into your home. On the way out of your bedroom, you confront a burglar who is coming towards you. He is built like a tank. You feel threatened and hit him with the club, breaking his arm and rendering him unconscious. The police arrive and charge you with assault. The burglar sues you for damages. You are convicted in Court and face going to jail and/or a massive fine.

Where did you go wrong?

Yes, someone had broken into your home.

Yes, he was bigger than you and you could therefore use an 'improvised' weapon.

Yes, he was coming towards you rather than running away from you so you would have felt threatened.

Yes, you would be allowed to defend yourself by hitting him with your golf club under these circumstances.

So why did you get sued and end up with a criminal conviction?

The simple reason is that you picked up the golf club you always kept by your bed in case you have a break-in. In other words, your actions were pre-meditated.

Now, if you were in bed when you heard a noise downstairs, you got up and on the way past your cupboard door, grabbed a golf club from your golf bag as an impromptu improvised weapon, then you never 'planned' to use this club so you are allowed to use it.

Yes, the burglar may still sue but under these circumstances he has no grounds to say that the way you defended yourself was unfair.

Yes, you will still be charged but, in this example, where you really did improvise a weapon, the Law will be on your side.

In fact, it is important to realise that you will probably **always** be charged when you are forced to defend yourself. It is not the police who decide if you are the aggressor or the victim, the attacker or the defender; they simply arrest and charge everyone involved.

It is then up to the judge and the jury to decide if you acted in self defence or not.

There is an old self defence saying that sums this sentiment up nicely;
"You are better to be judged by twelve than carried by six".

3.4 Making a Citizen's Arrest

I mentioned before that you could make a citizen's arrest and while this is your right, I do tend to advise people to think twice before using this option. Police Officers arrest people. They have handcuffs, CS gas spray, batons and in some countries, stun guns, tasers and/or firearms. They also have body armour and have been trained in arrest procedures. You have your bare hands. Leave the arresting to the police.

If that does not deter you, let me tell you what happened to father of two, Kevin Jackson, who chased after three men who were breaking into his father-in-law's car around Christmas 2001. Mr. Jackson resided in West Yorkshire, England, and had chased after the three men intent on making a citizen's arrest. He was soon overpowered however and one of the men used the screwdriver he had been using to break into the car to stab Mr. Jackson in the head. The others knocked him down with a tree branch and kicked him repeatedly before leaving him fatally injured in the street.

At the Court case, the man who stabbed Mr. Jackson said he had "poked" Mr. Jackson with the screwdriver in self defence. The jury did not believe this and all three men were jailed. Mr. Jackson was hailed as a 'have-a-go hero' by the media but was it worth it?

If you can avoid making a citizen's arrest, avoid it. Call the police and let them deal with it.

Don't be a dead hero!!

4. Self Defence training

It is important to evaluate the practical usefulness of any self defence programme before you sign up. Here are 3 tips:

4.1 Choosing an Instructor

1) Avoid martial arts clubs unless you specifically wish to train in traditional martial arts techniques. Most techniques taught will work well in a dojo or classroom environment where there are strict rules and regulations, but will rarely work in a street confrontation where there are no rules or referees. Many so called 'self defence programmes' teach variations on martial arts techniques. These are usually complex and difficult to remember under the stress of an actual attack.

2) The self defence programme you choose should revolve around simple but effective techniques designed to allow you to escape from an attack quickly. The programme should also include simulated assaults with a fully padded instructor who will put you through realistic rape (male and female) and attack scenarios thus allowing you to practice the simple techniques you've learned.

3) If you really want to see if your proposed self defence instructor is up to the job - see if their courses are recommended by your local Police. Most police forces will gladly recommend instructors who teach 'practical' self defence (usually incorporating the 'Bash & Dash' principle of self defence) but steer you away from the martial arts or the more dubious instructors. Recommended instructors will also be able to supply you with testimonials to support their training.

Security And Safety, for example, have testimonials from various UK police forces including London's Metropolitan Police, Scotland's Northern Constabulary and Strathclyde Police plus South Africa's Police Service as well as various military organisations including units of the UK's Royal Air Force, German and Greek Special Forces and civilian groups responsible for victims of abuse and/or attack including Women's Aid and Refuge, to name but a few.

**The author teaching a defensive open palm strike to a female
participant using B.O.B. (Body Opponent Bag)**

And the same open palm strike on a padded instructor

A padded Security And Safety instructor takes a strike to the face and a knee to the groin. Realistic attacks using padded instructors are a must for quality self defence course.

BOB takes another direct hit to the groin. He has had two tennis balls strategically placed for added effect. Women especially, get a huge sense of satisfaction seeing the balls fly off after a good knee to the groin!

The author teaches 5th and 6th year students alongside Scottish police officers. Note, the riot gear protection on the instructors' legs to enable students to kick with full force. Also note the police officer in the background being sent tumbling after a direct kick to the shins.

Attack scenarios need to be as realistic as possible. Instructors could use masks, fake knives, outside attacks – anything to make the class more varied and enjoyable.

Now this is not to say that I am knocking martial arts instructors or martial arts classes. There are plenty of martial arts instructors who are also fantastic self defence instructors – but there are also others who simply roll out what they know from their particular martial art and, as I have said in the introduction to this book, teaching a Karate 'Shito Ryu' manoeuvre or an 'Arae Makki' low forearm block used in Tae Kwon Do to stop a kick is not the best way to defend yourself.

Most martial arts classes will not cover personal awareness skills or the Law regarding self defence, reasonable use of force, etc.

That said, martial arts classes do have their place in preparing you to defend yourself. Practitioners do gain a huge amount of self confidence as they perform their techniques and katas. Speed and flexibility are also usually improved as certain exercises become instinctive. Strength can sometimes be increased as well as devastating techniques honed as participants learn to endure painful stances and become skilled at smashing through boards, bricks and tiles.

All of this will no doubt aid your defence if you are ever confronted by a would-be attacker. But remember that this attacker will not play by the rules of your martial art. You cannot cry "Foul" or expect a referee to stop the fight. So be prepared to fight dirty. To hit areas of an attacker's body that you would normally avoid in the dojo. But the first line of defence, unlike during a sparring match or competition, is to escape – FAST.

4.2 Escape

What if you are confronted by a knife wielding attacker who demands that you go with him? It may be in a car or into a deserted side street or into a hedgerow. It would seem prudent to do as you are told but it should be remembered that you are far more likely to be killed or seriously hurt if you go with your attacker than if you run away.

At the first opportunity - escape.

Run way, scream for help or better still shout "Fire". Research has shown that more people will come to your aid or to see what is going on if you shout "Fire" than if you shout "Help".

Do whatever you can to attract attention to yourself and your situation. Attackers do not want to be identified or disturbed, so let's not make it easy for them.

If your attacker is after your personal belongings be it your handbag, wallet, car keys or jewellery, let them have it by throwing it in the opposite direction to where you run.

If you think they are after you and not your belongings, be prepared to use anything you have on your person as an improvised weapon.

Coins in your pocket can be thrown in an attacker's face, a bag can be swung at an attacker's head, keys can be used to stab or slash, an umbrella can be used to hit out, shoes (especially high heels) can be used to hit at an attacker's face and head, etc.

4.3 The Defensive Stance

Feet shoulder width apart, knees slightly bent, arms up with palms open ready to push or strike your attacker. This is the defensive stance. Get ready to adopt it if you feel threatened and there is no way you can escape.

4.4 Voice control

After adopting the defensive stance, use your voice to control the situation. Remember I mentioned that if you defend yourself, you will be asked whether it was possible to prevent the attack using violence by non-violent means first. In other words, could you escape and did you try to warn your attacker off or talk to him?

We suggest that you try shouting "Get back" in an aggressive tone. Don't shout "Clear off" as this can be confused with "F**k off", both by witnesses and your attacker, and will only make matters worse.

"Get back" clearly states what you want to occur and threatens that you will do more if he does not comply.

So, why shout at all?

4 good reasons to shout

1. It means you comply with the Law.
2. It also has a psychological effect on your attacker. He wanted a helpless, vulnerable, easy victim. Now, he is faced with someone adopting a defensive stance. He may even think; "Oops, they must have done some form of martial art or self defence training to strike up a pose like this and they are shouting at me aggressively. I thought this was an easy target."

3. It may help you get witnesses. If anyone is close by they will turn around to see what is going on – and that is exactly what you want to show that you were defending yourself and not attacking.
4. It lets off a little bit of adrenalin from your body allowing you to control your actions and strength more effectively. Ever wonder why parachutists are taught to shout "Geronimo" or "1000, 2000, 3000, check canopy" when they can simply say this in their head to themselves? Or why are Karate martial artists taught to Kia? Your adrenalin builds up like steam in a kettle and shouting aggressively helps release a little of that pressure enabling you to focus.

4.5 Bodily weapons

Even if you were facing an attacker stark naked, you have 'weapons' to defend yourself. Your body is a weapon and if used correctly can be extremely effective – even deadly.

Here is a list of the various parts of your body that can be used and what you can use them for. This list is by no means conclusive but will hopefully give you a few ideas you perhaps never thought of before.

Hands: Push, Open Palm Strike, Punch, Hammer Blow, Slap, Power Slap, 'Karate' chop, Scratch, Poke.
Feet: Side kick, Heel kick.
Knees: Direct strikes or Roundhouse strikes.
Elbows: Direct strikes to the front or back or Roundhouse strikes.
Head: Forward head butt (Glasgow Kiss) or Backward head butt.

Hands

A simple Push can create enough space for you to get away from an attacker and if you can't push your attacker over, you could always push yourself off *him* to create this space.

But if you are going to get that close to an attacker, you really should be thinking of something that will stop him attacking you so I would suggest an Open Palm Strike. This is one of the most effective ways to defend yourself from the point of view of the Law regarding self defence.

Picture for a moment that you are about to be attacked; you raise your fists up and, after shouting at your would-be attacker to "Get Back", you punch him in the face. At your court case, witnesses say they couldn't quite make out what you shouted but confirmed that you shouted aggressively and held your hands in an aggressive manner. This is backed up by CCTV.

Now picture the same attack but this time with you holding your hands up ready for an open palm strike. The perception now is that you are holding your hands in a defensive pose. Take a look at the photos below and see what you think is a defensive and what is an aggressive pose.

You should never try to Punch your attacker unless you have been trained to do so as you will inevitably break the small bones in your fingers, perhaps even a few knuckles, and possibly sprain your wrist – leaving you defenceless after your first strike. Even professional boxers who punch all the time wear hand wraps that cover their wrists to avoid wrist sprains, so what chance have you got?

A Hammer Blow is great if your attacker is bent over and you deliver it to the nape of his neck or temple but it also works well if delivered to the sternum or side of neck or bridge of nose. Basically you form a fist but instead of striking with the knuckles, you strike with the padded side of the hand in a motion that resembles the wielding of a hammer.

A 'Karate' Chop is just like in the movies – the hand is kept flat and strikes the target with the fleshy side of the hand opposite the thumb. The problem is that this type of strike has limited usage in that it is really only effective when aimed at the neck or throat and this can be difficult in the heat of an attack.

So, what about a Slap and what is the difference between a Slap and a Power Slap? Well, a slap is just as it says. You have seen it many times on the TV and in the movies – the girl is about to be attacked and she slaps the attacker across his face. Effective? – Most definitely not!

A Power Slap uses the same principle as an ordinary slap but instead of the hand being flat when you make contact with your attacker, it is bent slightly almost as if you are cupping a handful of water.

This 'cupping' effect creates a little pocket of air when you make contact with the attacker and so adds a bit more power to the strike. I suggest aiming for the attacker's ear – the air pocket will be forced into his ear canal and will certainly disorientate him or may even burst his ear drum causing him severe pain. If not his ear, then his neck where several pressure points can be found and this too will effectively disorientate him.

Another seemingly ineffectual manoeuvre would be a Poke to the eyes. Yes, you could deliberately target the eyes in a finger strike – but again, this takes lots of practice and skill to be effective in a real fight where the attacker's head is moving.

More effective, particularly if grabbed by an attacker, is the Poke to the eyes using your thumbs. Combine this with the Power Slap and you get a devastating result.

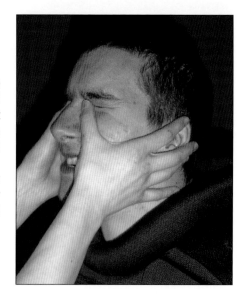

If you are tempted to scratch at your attacker's face, combine it with an open palm strike. If the attacker's face is still near your hand after this strike, your fingers will automatically drop into the eye sockets as your nails drag down his face. Very effective and you have lots of the attacker's DNA trapped in your fingernails to offer the police.

Feet

A good point to remember is that you should never kick above the knee in a street fight. It is far too easy for an attacker to grab your leg and break it or drag you off your feet into a bush where he can continue his attack.

The shin is full of nerve endings as you probably know – just think of the last time you bumped it against a coffee table. Now think of that pain intensified ten or twenty fold. The shin is such a painful area to get hit on and so difficult to defend that it was a prime target point for Special Forces troops being taught battlefield unarmed combat from World War II onwards. And if you don't believe me, take a look at "Kill or Get Killed" by Colonel Rex Applegate (first published in 1943 while he was working with the Office of Strategic Services (O.S.S.) then updated in 1976 with the help of the Combat Section, Military Intelligence Training Center, Camp Ritchie, Maryland).

A good hard kick to your attacker's shin will have him off balance immediately and hopping around in agony – that is if he is still standing.

Another point to remember though is never kick with the toe of your foot. You may break your toes and you are far more likely to miss your target than if you kicked with the inside of your foot (footballer style).

Knees

A knee to the groin is an obvious defensive strike and, due to the collection of nerve endings in the pubic bone area, can be just as effective on a female as it can on a male.

If upon kneeing your attacker in the groin, you find he is still standing, you can follow this up with a knee to the head as he is bent over.

If, on the other hand, your attacker was incapacitated on the ground after your first knee to the groin, you probably would not need to follow up your initial strike as he would no longer pose an immediate threat.

A Roundhouse Knee would see your knee striking the ribs and kidney area of an attacker and can be very effective if practiced however you need to remember to withdraw this strike quickly as you don't want your attacker to grab your knee and take the advantage.

Elbows

Elbows can be used in a variety of different moves to disable an attacker. The Downward Elbow Strike is ideal if your attacker is bent over (possibly after receiving a knee to the groin). You should aim for the nape of the neck in this position.

The Upward Elbow Strike can be as effective as an upper cut in western boxing however you need to have precision aiming to connect with the chin or nose of an attacker's head so this particular technique is not always ideal in the blur of a real attack.

The Roundhouse Elbow Strike is similar to the hook in western boxing only instead of connecting with the fist, you connect with your forearm as close to the elbow as possible. It's like getting hit with a metal bar across the face.

Another obvious use of the elbow is when being attacked from the rear. A quick succession of elbow strikes to your attacker's solar plexus should aid your escape.

If your arms and legs are pinned down, you can still use your head to get away. In Glasgow the Forward Head Butt is so common as an *initial* form of attack that it is known as the 'Glasgow kiss'. This reputation can be found in other cities and so you may know this particular technique as the 'Liverpool kiss' or the 'Manchester kiss'. Basically, it is a strike involving your forehead connecting with the nose or mouth area of your attacker.

The Backward Head Butt is when you have been grabbed from behind and you throw your head backwards to connect the back of your skull with your attacker's nose or mouth area.

4.6 The 'T' Zone

So, now that we have covered your own bodily weapons, where is the most effective areas to strike an attacker?

If you were the Prime Minister's bodyguard and someone was attacking him in front of TV cameras and press photographers, you really would not want to be involved in a fight where several punches are exchanged followed by a head butt and then some rolling around the ground before you finally stopped him. It would be far better if you could use one, perhaps two strikes to disable the attacker with minimal fuss. So how is this done?

Well, we always aim for the 'T' Zone in an attacker.

A strike anywhere in the 'T' Zone will have a far greater effect than anywhere else in the body.

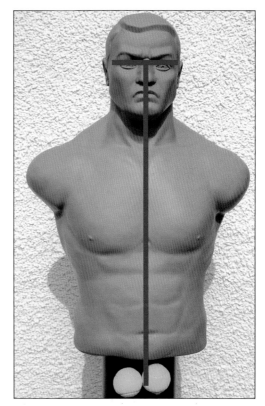

Ears

A Power Slap to the ears may cause concussion and could possibly burst an eardrum causing intense pain and loss of balance. A blow just behind the ear can cause shock to the cranial nerves and spinal cord resulting in concussion and temporary paralysis.

Eyes

A blow to this area can result in disorientation and severe watering of the eyes. The cheek bone may also fracture causing intense pain. Forcing a thumb into the eyes will have the same effects and will also result in temporary blindness.

Nose

A blow to the bridge of the nose could fracture it resulting in haemorrhaging, temporary blindness and severe watering of the eyes resulting in disorientation. A solid blow may also result in slight brain trauma leading to unconsciousness.

Lips

A blow to this area has the lips being forced into the teeth resulting in bleeding and involuntary giddiness.

Jaw

A light blow will result in the attacker's eyes watering and slight disorientation. A solid blow will cause the jaw to impact against the cranial nerves resulting in unconsciousness. The lower jaw and/or the cheek bones may also fracture.

Throat

A blow to this area will cause disorientation and severe eye watering and may also result in a restriction to the trachea due to swelling. Death is a possibility in this case and so should only be used if your life is in danger.

Sternum

A solid blow to this area could alter the heart's rhythm leading to temporary loss of breathing, unconsciousness and possibly death.

Solar plexus

A light but solid blow to this area will cause loss of breath and possible damage to internal organs. A hard, solid blow to this area can cause extreme pain and even death due to heart stoppage. In Dim Mak, the solar plexus is referred to as Conceptor Vessel 14 and is classed as *the* most forbidden point in acupuncture. It is also a common striking point in Taekwondo where it is used in a variety of attacks including 3 Step Sparring.

Groin

In a male, a blow to this area will cause loss of breath with severe pain and nausea. Ruptured testes will also induce vomiting and unconsciousness.

In males or females, a solid blow could fracture the pubic bone causing severe pain and nausea and probable splinters of bone entering the intestines or bladder.

Warning: The information given regarding target areas and techniques to stop an attacker should only ever be used in self defence. A blow to any of these areas is designed to give you enough time to escape from an attack. If you strike solid and hard, you should only need to hit out once to be effective and you should therefore rarely need to hit out to multiple target areas. You should never use this information in a sustained attack.

4.7 Attack scenarios

Here are a few attack scenarios to give you some ideas on the type of training you should be teaching and receiving. The scenarios are by no means conclusive – you could easily fill volumes of personal safety / self defence books just on different types of attack and that is precisely why you need to find a good instructor and practice with them over a long period of time.

For now though, I will concentrate on a few examples of attack;

Front Attack

Although this book is entitled "The Complete Book of Personal Safety" and not "The Complete Book of Self Defence" (which may be my next project), it is important to address a few practical 'what ifs', for instance, what if someone ignores your defensive stance and your aggressive "Get back" warning and comes at you, face on, with the intent on knocking your head from your shoulders?

As I have intimated, there are hundreds of techniques you can use to respond to this threat however the one technique preferred by most UK police forces is known as "Bash 'n' Dash" and is simply an advanced form of the 'police push' technique.

Not so long ago, police forces taught civilians how to get away from an attacker using what they described as a 'Police Push'. This was more a way for the victim to push themselves off their attacker as he advanced towards them rather than the victim trying to physically push their attacker away from them.

Unfortunately, this technique rarely works and an aggressive attacker would have succeeded in knocking your head off before you managed to push yourself away from him.

To make this technique effective you have to add in a kick to throw the attacker off balance.

A kick to the head is too risky, requires perfect timing and balance and cannot be mastered by everyone.

A kick to the groin is a little too high and could result in your leg being trapped by your attacker.

A kick to the shin however is virtually impossible to defend against and has fantastic results as the shin bone is covered in nerve endings and, if you have ever bumped your shin on a coffee table, is extremely painful if hit.

Think of the pain you felt after bumping against that coffee table and now treble that pain and you will begin to realise what it feels like to get a full blown kick to the shin.

I have already mentioned that Colonel Rex Applegate taught shin kicks to US Special Forces but so effective is this technique, that it was also taught by Major W.E. Fairburn (joint designer of the legendary Fairburn-Sykes fighting knife) to British and Canadian Special Forces personnel during World War II and is described in his book "Get Tough – How to Win in Hand-to-Hand Fighting".

If it works for soldiers in a battlefield, it will work for civilians in a street attack!

With that philosophy, UK police forces began to teach a simple shin kick followed by a 'push' or double open palm strike to the chest and/or head area. This technique is the "Bash 'n' Dash" technique shown in the photos below.

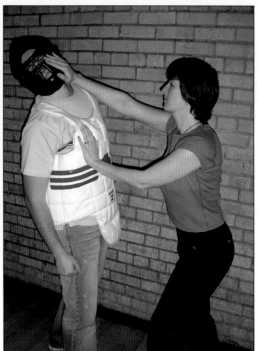
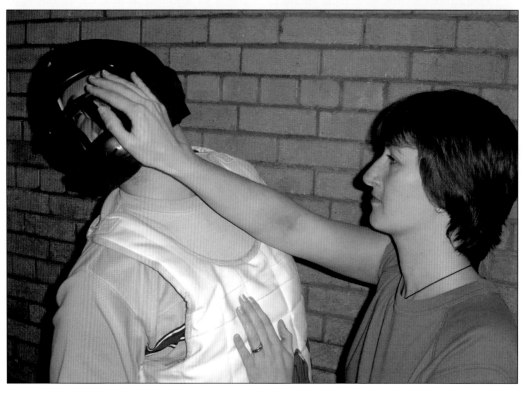

You will notice that the defender's foot is kicking like a footballer kicking a ball. It is side on to prevent the risk of missing the shin completely, which could easily occur if you tried kicking with the toes of the foot. Likewise, there is less chance of breaking a toe if you kick this way.

The attacker's body will automatically fall forward after being kicked in the shin allowing the defender, in this instance, to strike the chest and face with greater force (the force of the defender's strike plus the force of the attacker falling forward).

Having taught this technique to door stewards in Manchester, I got a telephone call informing me that this was now their preferred way of dealing with frontal attacks especially when the area they were working in is covered by CCTV.

The technique is clearly defensive as the other guy is charging towards them. They have simply put their hands up defensively then kicked him as hard as they could in the shin.

In most of the Manchester bouncer cases, the fight was apparently over with just the shin kick as the attacker's leg was invariably swiped from under him leaving him writhing in agony on the ground – all without a punch being thrown. Perfect! And to have the entire incident captured on CCTV for any Court to view is an added bonus.

There are obviously plenty of other techniques to stop a full frontal attack but as I mentioned earlier, this book deals with personal safety and a little self defence as opposed to self defence and a little personal safety. With that in mind, I will only cover a couple of techniques in various attack scenarios instead of a wide variety of techniques.

Strangle from the Front

Many martial arts / self defence books and courses will teach you how to break away from a front strangle such as the one illustrated, however most teach a variety of moves from a 'windmill' approach where your arms break free of the strangle (which can be effective if practised) to an upward break away motion as seen with dramatic effect in the movies (which is totally ineffective). The upward break away technique does not work in real life where an attacker has a firm grip on your throat and is actually strangling you!

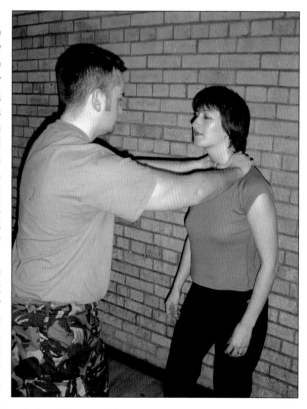

Don't believe me? Next time you are practising how to get out of a front strangle hold, ask your 'attacking' partner to actually strangle you (ensure you have a safety tap to signal to your partner when to let go before trying this). You will quickly find out that as an attacker applies pressure to your windpipe and throat, his arms will lock making an upward break-free impossible.

In fact the more you strike his arms upward, the more his arms will lock and then there is the added problem of your chin. An attacker who is squeezing the life out of you is doing so with his hands around your throat. You can try to force his hands up and over your chin but you will find that this too is not practicable, in fact the more you strike upwards the tighter he will contract his hands around your throat and the quicker you will lose consciousness.

The easiest way to get out of this strangle hold is to break *downwards* where your attacker's elbows naturally bend.

This has the double advantage of bending your attacker's body forwards and allowing your head (remember to tuck your own head down) to collide with his nose area.

Back Attack

Another common mistake made in most self defence courses and martial arts is to teach a specific method of escaping an attack from the back. This is often confusing because there is a difference between a grab from the back and the way you will be attacked from behind in the street.

Firstly, the normal method taught in most classes is as follows:

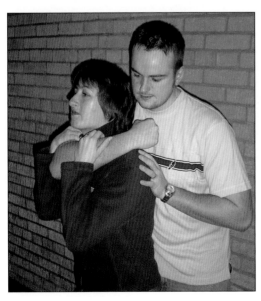 

Follow the elbow strike to the solar plexus with a heel kick to the shin and for extra effect, drag your heel down the shin (damaging nerves as you go down) and stamp your foot into the small bones of his foot. Brilliant!!

Well actually, not so brilliant!

You see, a back attack rarely happens like this in real life. Yes, you may get grabbed like this and have time to then perform your elbow strike etc. but why would an attacker run up to you, grab you from behind and hold you there?

Back attacks are split into two categories: violent physical attacks and sexually or other motivated attacks.

If it is a violent physical attack from behind, you will be hit to the ground and kicked or struck until you are unconscious or dead. Pity you were not a little more aware of your surroundings; you could have at least turned around to face your attacker thereby allowing yourself some chance of self defence!

Sexually or other motivated (possibly a mugging) back attacks will require the attacker to grab you and then drag you backwards to an area that is quieter, perhaps a bush or a less well lit area out of the way of passers-by, where he can continue his attack without fear of being disturbed.

Just one more reason to find out how to improve your own personal safety and to learn effective 'reality based' self defence techniques.

So, how exactly does a sexually or other motivated back attack occur?

It usually happens like this:

In the photograph, you will notice that the attacker has grabbed the victim around the neck, stopping them from screaming but more importantly cutting off their air supply. Instinctively, the victim will grab the arm causing the blockage so elbow strikes, throwing the attacker over your shoulder, etc., are all out the window now.

As the attacker walks backwards you will be tempted to heel kick him in the shin but all this will do is aid him in 'walking' you to the nearest bush or dark alleyway.

So, how do you get out?

You drop like a stone. Even Arnold Schwarzenegger cannot curl 8 stone or more in bodyweight with one arm so your attacker's body will bend forwards as you drop.

By tilting your head back you can now drop onto your back, cover your head in case your attacker recovers quickly enough to try to kick you, spin around and kick out at his shins and knees.

There are many advantages to the position you are now in;

1. If an attacker wanted to drag you back to a quieter area, would he continue with his attack now that you are lying down in the same area he grabbed you?
2. You (the victim) can now see your attacker's face, perhaps identify him but certainly able to describe him to the police later. Would the attacker continue his attack now?
3. You can also scream now. Something the attacker had prevented before with his choke hold. This may alert other people who will also become witnesses and may also be able to describe the attacker. Would the attacker still continue his attack?
4. And to make matters worse for the attacker, you are now in a better position to defend yourself and can begin to kick out at him.

This victim was chosen because it was presumed they were vulnerable, weak, easy prey. Now they are kicking and screaming like a warrior from "Braveheart". With so many things going wrong for him, do you really think the attacker would continue his attack?

Well, I honestly don't believe that he would but for arguments sake, let's say he does. But unlike the police officer in one of the earlier photos, he does not fall backwards when kicked on the shin, but falls forwards, on top of you.

How do you get out of this?

Ground attacks

When an attack ends up on the ground, some victims feel that it is all over for them. They have lost the fight. In actual fact, you are closer to winning. If your attacker keeps his distance, only coming close to you to strike at you and then moving away again, you will find it very hard to defend yourself and win the fight. The closer your attacker gets to you the easier it is to strike out at him and the quicker you can put him out of action.

If your attacker is on top of you there are a number of techniques you can utilise to get him off. Here are a couple;

The Hair Pull

Very simple! Grab your attacker's hair and yank it back to expose his throat. Bear in mind, he has now attacked you and got you on the ground; you really don't want to wait to see what he does next; your life is in danger. Strike out at his throat until he gets off you. If that is too aggressive for the situation you are in, place your hand on his throat and push. He will move off although this will not stop him and you may have to have a counter measure to stop him trying to get back on you again.

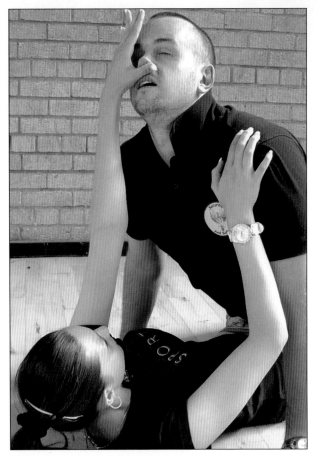

If he has no hair, place the edge of your thumb or index finger on the bridge of his nose and push upwards at an angle of about 45 degrees.

This technique is called the **'Nose Hook'** and is effective whether you have an attacker on top of you and you want him off or you have an attacker threatening you and you want to get away.

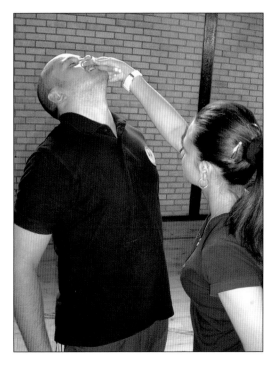

Working as a door steward, I once had to put out a drunken squaddie who was in a pub with a bunch of his soldier mates. Knowing that his mates would pounce on me if I got into a fight with the drunk, I had to show his mates that I was almost superhuman so I raised my index finger and made a point of telling them to "Stay where you are. Your mate has been warned and now he is leaving". I then lined him up with the exit, placed my index finger under his nose with my knuckle on the cleft between his nose and lips (see the above photograph) and marched him out quickly. He was outside before he knew it.

Coming back in again, I waved my index finger to the rest of the army boys saying "Behave" and hopefully made them think to themselves "Blimey, if he can put our mate out with one finger, what can he do with the other nine?"

The trick is to push on the piece of cartilage between his nostrils (the septum) at an angle of 45 degrees. If you push in at his lips instead of up, there will be little or no effect.

If you are being attacked however, you may not want to be as 'nice' so instead of *placing* your index finger under the bridge of his nose, you would strike him there with the opposite side of your index finger.

Don't worry about missing his septum, you should manage to strike his throat or chin area if not his nose – either way, he is going down!

If you are being attacked however, you may not want to be as 'nice' so instead of *placing* your index finger under the bridge of his nose, you would strike him there with the opposite side of your index finger. (See top two photos on the following page.)

The nose hook has many uses and causes extreme, localised pain to the attacker without causing any permanent damage (unless of course you strike him hard in which case you will probably burst his nose open perhaps even breaking it).

It can even be used to escape from choke holds and head locks;

The Head Twist

You may decide to utilise the head twist technique whereupon you place one hand on the back of your attacker's head and one hand on his chin. Like a giant corkscrew, you turn his head as though you want to take his chin from a six o'clock setting to nine o'clock. Don't push the head back, just turn it.

Warning: If you are practicing this technique, *do it slowly*. Performed quickly this could break your opponent's neck.

Sexual Attacks

What happens if your attacker has got you onto the ground and is now intent on continuing his attack on top of you? Obviously, if this was just a physical assault, the attacker could simply stand over you and rain kicks down onto you. If the attacker gets on top of you, it is more likely to be a sexual assault.

Do sexual assaults take place on a regular basis? Here are some facts for you to consider;

- One in three women will be sexually assaulted in her lifetime.
- One in three girls and one in five boys will be sexually assaulted by age 18. Nearly 85% will be abused by someone known to them.
- It is estimated that only 20% of all sexual exploitation cases involving the handicapped are reported to any agency.
- Every minute 1.3 reported rapes occur in the United States of America.
- In 50% of the families where physical violence occurs, the children are also sexually abused.
- On average, rapists sexually assault 50 times before they are caught. [15]

If your attacker is carrying out a sexual assault and has both your hands pinned down and his full body weight on top of you, your brain will be crying out to get him off and you will have an overwhelming desire to struggle. After a few minutes however your strength will have been depleted dramatically and when the attacker removes his hand from you in order to undo his trousers or remove your clothing, your strikes at him will be totally ineffective. Why?

Well, we all have adrenalin flowing through our bodies and in times of stress we have an increase of this hormone. This increase of adrenalin basically gives us a burst of energy and strength to either fight or flight – fend off an attacker or run away.

A perfect example of this surge of superhuman strength occurred in Afghanistan on the 5th November 2006 when Royal Marine Colour Sergeant Carl 'Tatts' Tatton braved Taliban mortar fire to lift a two ton truck off his injured comrade, by himself, despite the truck being over thirteen times his body weight.

His fellow Marine, Mark Farr, became trapped under the truck when a mortar bomb exploded near to the water filled ditch he was working in, flipping the truck down the bank and on to his leg.

---

[15] Rape Crisis, Intervention & Prevention, 2008

The two ton truck flipped on its side

As he lay injured and now drowning in the three foot water filled ditch, and with mortar shells still raining down, Mark must have thought he had only seconds to live but then Carl leapt into the ditch to try to free him.

Colour Sergeant Carl Tatton

This stressful situation gave Carl a powerful adrenalin surge that helped him perform the superhuman feat of lifting the two ton truck off his comrade.

The problem with this surge of hormone is that it usually only lasts around thirty seconds and then it rapidly decreases leaving your muscles drained of energy. This is know as the 'Adrenalin Dump'. If you have ever been in a fight or heated argument, you may have noticed your hands shaking afterwards and lifting anything is an effort. That is the adrenalin dump.

Now picture that 'dump' during a full blown attack. You struggle to get your attacker off you, your get an extra adrenalin boost to help you, but after resisting for around thirty seconds, you feel weak and there is no power left in your body. When he moves to undo his trousers, you see an opportunity to hit him in the face but the resulting strike merely glances off him and does not appear to cause him any damage or pain.

Unfortunately, this is a familiar scenario to police officers dealing with rape victims. The rapist knows your adrenalin will dump leaving you weak and, in fact, is counting on it.

It is estimated that in 2003 approximately 50,000 women were raped in the UK, however only 12,760 reported this to the police. Of those cases, 1,649 went to trial but, shockingly, only 673 resulted in successful prosecutions. If you reported a rape in the UK in 2003 you had a mere 5.3% chance of getting your rapist convicted.[16]

In 2007, the Home Office released its latest figures on rape convictions and confirmed that only around 6% of all reported rape offences resulted in a conviction.

Worst still, speaking at a Rape Crisis Scotland conference in 2008, the Scottish Lord Advocate, Elish Angiolini, confirmed that only 3.9% of reported rapes in Scotland end in conviction.

Unfortunately, these statistics only confirm that nothing has changed from a legal proceedings / convictions point of view. In fact, in 2007 it was confirmed that the UK now has the lowest conviction rate in the EU for rape. [17]

So if the legal system cannot help you, you may have to help yourself.

Your attacker has got you on the ground and knows your adrenalin will dump soon after you begin to struggle. How do you get out of this attack?

If your martial arts / self defence instructor teaches how to evade this form of attack, and most don't cover sexual attacks, you will probably find that they simulate the attack by having the 'attacker' hold the 'victim' down by the arms only. In reality, the attacker usually uses his entire bodyweight to pin the victim to the ground.

Your adrenalin will have undoubtedly kicked in by now and your instinct will be to get this attacker off you. But what you won't realise is that adrenalin does not last forever – as previously mentioned, perhaps up to half a minute if you are lucky – and then it slowly ebbs away leaving your muscles extremely weak.

[16] Her Majesty's Inspectorate of Constabulary & Her Majesty's Crown Prosecution Service Inspectorate (2007)
[17] Rape Convictions as a Proportion of Recorded Rape Offences: House of Commons Library, 2007

Serial rapists and attackers know this and know that, at this stage, they could let both your hands go and your strikes would be virtually ineffective.

Many rape victims have blamed themselves for 'freezing' or being 'unable' to fend an attacker off. In reality, their body would not let them as it was physically spent; rendered weak by their adrenalin dump.

So, how can you prevent this happening?

Hopefully you will never be in this situation but if you are, remember this advice; STOP FIGHTING. You are only wasting your energy and the extra adrenalin you have by trying to get your attacker off you at this stage. His bodyweight and strength may be too great for you to win – so don't even try.

By going limp, you will be able to assess the situation clearer while keeping your adrenalin in reserve. Your attacker will think that your adrenalin has dumped and you are now tired and weak (as has happened to so many of his other victims) and so he is now free to loosen his trousers, pull at your skirt or trousers and carry on the sexual stage of his attack.

You are waiting for that opening where you can do the most damage.

As soon as your attacker takes his weight off your body and perhaps even lets go of one of your arms to undo his trousers, strike him with all the force you can muster.

Slide the arm that is still trapped upward along the ground so that your bent arm is now straightening. Your attacker will slide along with it because the majority of his bodyweight is on this arm.

As he loses his balance, strike his face or throat with your free hand to throw him off you at the same time as straightening your trapped arm fully.

Once he is off you, continue to strike him in the face area with elbows, forearms and hands until he no longer moves and you can escape.

Ground attack from the rear

The worst case scenario would be a ground attack where you are face down instead of on your back. Sometimes this occurs because you have been knocked down or tripped up as part of a mugging but this is also a common position for sexual attacks – particularly sexual attacks on males.

As before, the attacker will usually place his entire bodyweight on top of you.

As before, you need to stop struggling and wait for your opening.

This time, because you are facing down into the ground, you can tilt your body to fire the elbow of your freed arm into your attacker's face at the same time as extending your trapped arm to throw him off balance.

Keep firing your elbow and hands into his face and throat area until he stops attacking you and you can escape. Don't be a statistic!

4.8 'Improvised Weapons' for defending yourself

A self defence aid such as a personal attack alarm can be a useful weapon. When they first hit our streets back in the early eighties the siren was loud enough to attract the attention of passers-by however as technology grew and car alarms began to go off every few minutes, these personal attack alarms began to get ignored. It was then that the shift came from an alarm to attract attention to a self defence tool that could disorientate your attacker.

The decibel output of a modern personal attack alarm is around 130 decibels – that's the equivalent of a jackhammer going off next to you (normal conversation is around 60 decibels with shouting being 80 decibels and even a chainsaw is only 120 decibels). Pull the safety pin and point the alarm at an attacker and he will find it difficult to continue his attack as the high sound frequency disturbs the equilibrium of his inner ear.

Sounds great, however it is important to understand that there can be drawbacks to its use.

If you are carrying it in your handbag, for example, you will not only waste time trying to locate it but you will likely alert the attacker to your intentions while you fumble for it.

Various other 'improvised weapons' can be found on your person and can easily be used to stop an attacker or give you a few vital seconds to escape – as long as you make sure they are handy;

- Your keys (used to stab if a Mortise key or slash if a Yale key)
- Belt buckle (wrapped around your hand as an improvised knuckle duster or a swinging weapon similar to the Manriki Gusari used in ancient Japan)
- Shoes (especially high heels used to aid a strike)
- Your coat (to throw over and disorientate an attacker giving you a chance to escape)
- Coins (to throw at an attacker's face)
- A rolled magazine/newspaper (when used as a stabbing 'weapon' a rolled up newspaper can smash through a plate glass window)
- Hairspray or perfume in your handbag (sprayed into the eyes of an attacker should give you time to escape)
- An umbrella (again used in a stabbing motion)

The list is almost endless. But never *solely* depend on any self defence aid or 'improvised weapon' to stop an attacker. Learn to defend yourself using your own body and your wits.

5. Daily Personal Safety

Hopefully being aware of your surroundings will prevent any form of attack or robbery occurring to you personally but part of being aware is being aware of the different forms of violent or threatening behaviour you can face daily;

5.1 Mugging & Pick Pocketing

Any robbery that occurs in the street is usually known as a mugging whether it be a snatch and grab or being held up at knife point. Muggings most often occur in quiet dark areas. You would be forgiven for thinking that young women or the elderly would be high on the list of a mugger but, strangely enough, young men tend to suffer more muggings than anyone else and more frequently incur injuries while being mugged. Perhaps this is due to the fact that young men tend to carry more money on a night out than any other demographic.

If anyone approaches you in the street and demands money, threatening violence, just surrender it to them. It's only money! You only have one life – don't let them take that as well.

By contrast, pick pocketing occurs in busy, people dense areas such as an underground train station during rush hour. This is because a good pickpocket needs to have a lot of bodies brushing against you in order to desensitise you and therefore render you unaware that you are being robbed.

5.2 Bigotry

People are different in many ways and most of us can easily live with each other without giving religion, race or sexuality a second thought. There are however some people out there who literally hate other people because of who or what they are. It may be because they belong to an ethnic minority or because they have a different religion or because their sexual preferences are different.

Acts of bigotry can often be seen as racism or hate crimes or sectarianism and can involve verbal abuse, insulting graffiti, hate mail and even physical assault.

If you are the victim of bigotry, remember it is not your fault. Everyone has the right to live their life the way they want to. That is why we live in a democratic country. Police officers are now trained to recognise and deal with race, religion and sexually motivated crime. If you are a victim, report it.

5.3 Bogus Callers

Criminals will use every trick in the book to gain access to your home, whether you are out or in. Never open your door unless you are either certain you know who's on the other side or you can verify that they have a legitimate reason for being there.

Bogus callers may resort to dressing up - from everything from a repair person from the Gas Board to a Police Officer checking you home security. If in doubt, check them out. Ask them for identification and call their boss to make doubly sure that they are not bogus callers.

In the event of an intruder breaking in while you are at home, you should have a 'safe room' in your house to which you can retreat to. This room should have a strong door with a deadbolt lock and contain a telephone (preferably a mobile). Most people will find that this 'safe room' is their toilet or bathroom.

Be prepared to use seemingly everyday items as 'improvised weapons' so that you can get away from your attacker / intruder. The list is again endless but here are a few examples;

Kitchen: Rolling pin, pots & pans, kettle, kettle cord, boiling water, fire extinguisher, salt / pepper. Pepper spray may be illegal to buy in this country but you can legally make up your own, perhaps for use in stir-fries (??) – a couple of ounces of curry powder plus a couple of ounces of pepper in ½ pint of warm water. Put into a spray bottle, keep it somewhere handy and 'hey presto' an effective deterrent to be used against any attacker. You will get similar effects with washing powder mixed with water in a spray bottle.
Note: Due to the potentially lethal damage they can cause, knives are not seen as a good option for self defence but can be used if your life is threatened.

Lounge: Poker, golf clubs (if you are the sporty type), rolled up newspaper, pen/pencil, ashtray, standard lamp, flower pot.

Bathroom: Soap bar wrapped in a towel to use as an improvised cosh, aerosol sprays, toilet brush, toilet roll stand, toothbrush (to aim at the 'T' or pressure points such as the underarm, triceps or thighs).

Bedroom: Socket end of bedside lamp, socket end of an alarm clock, Dressing gown (to throw over and disorientate attacker).

6. Personal Safety when Socialising

There are many occasions when you should actively consider your personal safety; at work if you work alone or in a high risk field, when walking in quiet or deserted areas, if you stay alone at home, etc. but the area of personal safety that most often gets neglected is when you are socialising.

We tend to want to have a good time when we are socialising – have fun, maybe have a few drinks, meet up with friends – and under these circumstances, we can often forget about our own personal safety.

Simple precautions can help such as checking your surroundings, walking in open well lit locales, avoiding shortcuts through isolated areas, travelling in groups if going out at night, displaying confident alert body language, etc.

But sometimes we can be caught off guard and hopefully this section of the book will focus your mind on why your personal safety should never be forgotten.

6.1 'Date rape' drugs

Unfortunately, so called 'date rape' drugs are becoming increasingly common both in the UK and abroad. There are four main groups of drugs used in 'date rape':

- **Clonazepam** (known as Klonopin in the USA and Rivotril in Mexico)
- **Ketamine** (ketamine hydrochloride)
- **GHB** (gamma-hydroxybutrate) and **GBL** (gamma-butyrolactone) – both also known as 'Liquid Ecstasy' and 'GHB'.
- **Benzodiazepines** (including Rohypnol (flunitrazepam), Valium and Xanax).

Up until around 2008 the most common 'date rape' drug used in the UK was Rohypnol. It is still the most common in other parts of the world where it is more readily available.

The pharmaceutical company Hoffman-La Roche Inc. produces Rohypnol and sells it in Latin America, South America, Europe, Africa, the Middle East and Asia however it is difficult to obtain legally in the UK and the USA.

Rohypnol has physiological effects similar to Valium (diazepam) but is approximately *ten times more potent* and is known by several street names: Roachies, Roofies, Ruffies, Rophies, Roche, La Roche, Rope, Rib, Mexican valium or the "Forget Me pill."

In the early days of 'date rape', Rohypnol pills could be easily identified if you saw them. They were white, scored on one side, with the word "ROCHE" and an encircled with a number 1 or 2 (depending on the dosage) on the other.

Between 1996 and 1997 the pills with the encircled '2' were phased out by Hoffman-La Roche Inc. and they plan to phase out the one milligram variety in the near future bringing out an olive green, oblong tablet with the number 542 scored on it instead. This tablet contains a dye which turns drinks green if dissolved in them and is a valiant effort by the company to stop its illegal use.

Unfortunately, these original legal drugs have now been copied by illegal drug cartels and are very cheap to buy on the street with pills selling for as little as £1 or $1.

When used in a 'date rape', Rohypnol is often dissolved in a drink and when this happens it is undetectable. You can't see it, you can't smell it and you can't taste it.

Rapists and attackers will use this drug because it makes their victim unable to resist an assault.

When ingested, Rohypnol takes effect within ten minutes. The victim may feel dizzy and disoriented, simultaneously too hot and too cold, or nauseated. They will want to leave the safety of the club or bar that they are in so as to get back to their home or hotel. This is when the attacker will strike.

The drug takes full effect within thirty minutes, peaks within two hours, and can persist for up to eight hours. It can induce a blackout with memory loss and a decrease in resistance. Usually victims experience difficulty speaking and moving, and then pass out. Such victims have no memories of what happened while under the drug's influence.

Since 2008 however, the favoured date rape drug in the UK has become GBL simply because it is still legal to buy.

GHB on the other hand is a Class C drug in the UK. It is illegal to possess it (up to two years in jail and/or an unlimited fine) and illegal to supply someone else either by selling or by giving to friends. Supplying can get you up to 14 years in jail and/or an unlimited fine. - and this is why the majority of users in the UK are turning to GBL.

The Advisory Council on the Misuse of Drugs (ACMD) which advises the Government, considers that the harms of GBL and 1,4-BD (which is a similar, lesser-known chemical) are equal to other Class C drugs. The Government therefore intends to control GBL and 1,4-BD as Class C drugs by the end of 2009 however, as it is a chemical used in industry, it will continue to be available for legitimate users.

Any drug used to assist a sexual assault in the UK comes under the the Sexual Offences Act 2003 as it states that it is "an offence to administer a substance to a person with intent to overpower that person to enable sexual activity with them". This is punishable by up to 10 years imprisonment – but it does not seem to be much of a deterrent.

The age range of date rape victims is varied from teenagers to senior citizens.

Worst of all is that all of these 'date rape' drugs will leave the victim's system within 72 hours of ingestion and cannot be detected in any routine toxicology screen or blood test. So if the victim waits to recover from the effects of the drug and then the shock of the rape, it is likely that they have very little time left to report this to the police and have them identify the drug used.

All 'date rape' drugs have similar effects as described above for Rohypnol. None of them have any taste, odour or colour and dissolve in liquid without a trace.

To avoid becoming a victim of rape under the influence of these drugs try to follow a few simple rules:

- Be wary about accepting drinks from anyone you don't know well or long enough to trust.
- If you are accepting a drink, make sure it's from an unopened container and that you open it yourself.
- Don't put your drink down and leave it unattended, even to go to the toilet.
- Stay alert and be aware of your surroundings.

These tips may seem drastic but so are the possible alternatives. In 2007, more than 1000 women in Britain reported being raped while drugged[18] – and remember, just because very few men report being assaulted or raped while drugged does not mean it is not happening. It just means men find it harder to admit and report.

6.2 Bogus Taxis

Most people are aware that in the UK there are two types of taxis - Hackney Carriages or 'black cabs' (which can be hailed or picked up at a taxi rank) and Private Hire cars which operate within a controlled area. Both types of taxi are thoroughly checked by the authorities before a 'sealed' vehicle licence plate is granted, giving them the right to 'ply for hire' in their controlled area. The potential taxi driver will also undergo a strict knowledge exam of their chosen area of operation (3 to 4 years to obtain a Green 'all London' Badge) and are, in the case of the bigger companies, CRB checked.

---

[18] Home Health UK Ltd, 2008

However there is another 'type' of taxi driving through our streets – the bogus taxi. Here are a few personal safety tips to avoid the bogus taxi:

1. Try to pre-book your taxi or private hire vehicle via their office. Never hail a taxi from the street – unless it's a Hackney Carriage. You have no idea whether or not the car is licensed (unless you have confirmed this by the taxi registration plate on the rear bumper) and you don't know if the driver is a registered taxi driver or not.
2. Take a taxi business card or write down the telephone number of a taxi company you know or have used before in the past. Alternatively, walk to the nearest taxi cab office or pick one up at a taxi rank. Don't just flag one down.
3. If you don't have the number of a taxi company, ask the staff in the pub or club you are in to recommend one.
4. Try not to let anyone overhear you ordering a taxi as they may simply leave and come back in again pretending to be your taxi driver.
5. If possible, ask for the driver's name, the make and colour of the taxi which will be sent for you and check all of this upon its arrival. Remember that 'professional' bogus taxi drivers listen to the radio transmissions of taxi firms, so may know your name and destination. One thing they cannot replicate though is the make, model and colour of the car the taxi firm is sending you – so be sure to ask and ensure it is the real taxi you are getting into.
6. When the taxi arrives, make sure the driver asks for you by your name. Don't ask the driver if he is your taxi.
7. Check the taxi has a taxi registration plate on the rear bumper.
8. If you are suspicious, check that the registration plate matches the license plate of the taxi.
9. If the driver does not have his identity badge displayed, ask to see it before getting in.
10. Check the destination the driver has been given for you.
11. Always sit in the back of the taxi.
12. If you chat with your taxi driver, try not to give away any personal details about you – are you single, do you live alone, etc.
13. If you are at all suspicious about your driver, ask him to stop at a busy or familiar place and get out.
14. Have your door keys ready for when you arrive at your destination and be prepared to use them as an 'improvised weapon' if you are attacked.
15. When you get to your destination, ask the driver to wait until you are inside.
16. Never fall victim of the taxi driver who shouts "Taxi, love?" or "Did someone call a taxi?" These are typical ploys used by bogus taxi drivers. If you are approached in this way, ignore them. Touting is an offence in the UK. Taxi drivers who tout for business will have their details, fingerprints and DNA recorded by police.

There are many dangers connected to unlicensed taxis and private hire vehicles, some more obvious than others.

Unlicensed vehicles won't have been examined by local authorities for safety and roadworthiness. They may not have vehicle insurance let alone passenger insurance and they may not even have an MOT.

The driver won't have went through the rigorous qualifications that a licensed driver is subjected to so you may find that he doesn't even have a driving licence – or if he has that he has been disqualified for drink driving or has numerous speeding / driving convictions. He may even have more serious criminal convictions that would normally preclude him from becoming a taxi driver such as sexual assault, rape or offences involving violence.

And if you think this is unlikely, you may be shocked to find out that there are over 200 taxi-related assaults and rapes each year **in London alone**. Almost all of these are by bogus taxi drivers and Metropolitan Police estimate the actual number of taxi-related assaults could be ten fold.[19]

6.3 Public transport

You will be safest when you are with other people so try not to travel alone, especially at night.

Ensure you have planned your route in advance. Asking for directions to bus stops or train stations will only get you noticed. Likewise asking directions of your fellow travellers for example, "Can you tell me when we get to Princes Street bus stop?" will also attract the attention of a potential attacker.

When you get onto your bus or train, try to sit in a well lit area, near to other people. If you are on a bus, the driver is the best person to sit near to. If you are on a train, try to sit next to the conductor.

If anyone makes you feel uncomfortable or your 'sixth sense' or 'women's intuition' tells you something is wrong, move to a different part of the bus or even a different carriage if on a train.

6.4 Travel & Hotel Safety

Always remember, wherever you travel to and wherever your hotel is located, your safety is paramount. More and more adventure holidays are on offer to people. At the same time, murders, kidnappings, muggings, hotel break-ins and other crimes are also on the increase. So it's important that everyone, but especially women, keep in mind the following security and safety tips while travelling and staying in hotels:

- Always purchase travel insurance before heading off. This will give you the added security of knowing that you are only a phone call away from medical, security or travel-related assistance should you require it.
- Travel light. Women should wear comfortable, flat shoes so that they can move quickly through terminals.
- Always stay alert. If your head is buried in a book or you are walking with earphones on listening to your iPod, you will be unaware of your surroundings and vulnerable to an attack.
- Watch for people brushing against you in crowds. This is often a technique used by pick pockets who frequent airport, train and bus terminals.
- Whenever possible, make arrangements to arrive before dark.
- If you have arranged for transportation at the airport, instead of having your name on a placard, agree upon an object or password that is known only to you and the driver/company picking you up.
- Don't get into the bad habit of using your business card as a luggage tag. And don't show off your prestigious credit card or designer tags that provide more information than is absolutely necessary - thieves look for tags they recognise.
- Use valet parking whenever possible. Self-park only in well-lit areas. Ask for an escort to your car if valet parking is not available.
- Keep some money in an outside pocket to avoid fumbling through your purse or wallet for tips and other expenses.

---

[19] Project Sapphire, Metropolitan Police, 2007

- When you get to your accommodation, request a room on a lower, but not the ground floor in your hotel. Ground floor rooms are easily reached by criminals while rooms above the sixth floor may have a nice view but are too high for most fire fighting equipment to reach.
- If you have been out and about and you phone for a taxi, ask the driver to come and find you. Don't offer your name - wait for the cabby to tell you who he is here to pick up. That way you can be sure he is from the company you called and not a bogus driver (See the 'Bogus Taxis' section for more tips).
- Also request that your room door has a peephole, dead bolt and chain lock. And make sure it has no connecting door to another room.
- Never stay in a hotel with 'hard' keys. Hotels with security cards are much safer as the cards are destroyed after use. 'Hard' keys have a habit of being duplicated and passed around.
- Try to select a hotel known for taking extra measures to ensure personal security. If you cannot do this, remember most hotel room locks are not secure.
- Purchase a small, inexpensive door alarm and use it when travelling. (Most personal attack alarms can be easily converted to door alarms.) You may also want to purchase a rubber door jam. Again, they are inexpensive and will provide you with extra security.
- Once in your room, check where the nearest fire exits are and physically open the fire doors to see where they lead to. They could be blocked or locked or they may lead to a wall ladder - remember, it may be dark and smoky the next time you use it, so check it out and get your bearings.
- Take a small torch with you on your trip. Having a torch will make it easier for you to find your way out if the power goes off in the event of an emergency.
- Never give out your room number. If a clerk announces it out loud, request a room change.
- Never let anyone who is unidentified into your room. Always confirm who they are through the view-hole, if possible. Likewise, if you have to meet people on business, do not invite them to meet you in your room. Meet in a public location, such as the hotel lobby, restaurant or bar.
- If you're expecting take-out food or a package from outside the hotel, have it delivered to the front desk or concierge. Many hotel attacks happen from bogus delivery men.
- Ask to have a five-minute warning phone call before room service or other deliveries are sent to your room.
- An unusual but very effective tip for women travelling alone is to bring a man's shirt or a pair of men's boxer shorts with you. Before answering the door to your hotel room put the article of clothing on your bed, turn on the shower and close the bathroom door - your visitor will think you're not alone.
- When leaving your hotel room, leave the "do not disturb" sign on your door and turn your TV onto the local language station. Any unwelcome guests will assume you are in and are a local.
- If travelling to a country with a high crime rate (statistics and information are available from the Foreign Office), buy plastic connectors that you can place on your luggage bags when leaving your room. It won't prevent someone from opening your bags, but it will tell you if someone has opened them and taken something. It will also tell you if someone has opened them to place something in your bags - remember, some countries have a large degree of drug smuggling and single travellers are ideal targets to hide drugs in their bags.
- Where possible, avoid taxis. You cannot be sure that they are legitimate and even if they are you cannot be sure that the driver has been fully checked out. Remember,

even in New York City 90% of Yellow Cab drivers are recently arrived immigrants.[20] Have they all been through a Police check? To ensure your safety, ask your hotel's concierge to recommend a driver or car service.

- If you do decide to take a taxi, don't volunteer information about your trip, its duration or its purpose to your driver. It's nobody's business but your own.
- Don't advertise your nationality. Wearing a trendy T-shirt such as "I love N.Y." not only announces your origins but can also attract the wrong kind of attention. Try to look like everyone else.
- Always stay aware of your surroundings and the people around you - even when sight seeing. Scams on unsuspecting travellers often begin with someone trying to distract their attention. Be aware that scam artists often work in pairs or groups and use distractions to give them time to pick pocket tourists.
- Always keep a clear head. Restrict or avoid drinking alcohol especially if someone buys you a drink. The number of incidents of spiked drinks are on the increase, especially the use of the so called 'date rape drugs'. (See the 'Date Rape Drugs' section for further details).

Many hotels in the USA have already taken measures to meet women travellers' needs. The Pan Pacific San Francisco for example supplies female guests with a personal escort to their room and each room is equipped with an emergency help button to be used in case of attack or emergency.

Some hotels in Australia, the USA and in now in London also set aside 'networking tables' in their restaurants for solo travellers who prefer to eat with others. Some hotels also provide business lounges with space for safe, neutral meetings.

And in some USA and Japanese hotels, exercise conscious guests can even hire a jogging partner. These running escorts for joggers are sometimes included in exclusive hotels on a complimentary basis and the service includes chilled bottled water, fresh fruit and a plush towel upon return.

[20] Schaller, 1992

7. Domestic Violence

Some people may be unfamiliar with the term 'domestic violence' but will recognise the term 'domestic abuse'. By expressing this specific act as 'violence' instead of 'abuse' highlights the importance the UK Government, law officials and aid agencies have put on its impact and consequences.

The UK Government definition of domestic violence was agreed in 2004 and is;

"Any incident of threatening behaviour, violence or abuse (psychological, physical, sexual, financial or emotional) between adults who are or have been intimate partners or family members, regardless of gender or sexuality."

This definition can include forced marriages and so-called 'honour crimes'.

Although this behaviour has now been termed as domestic 'violence', not all the behaviour in this category need be physically 'violent' e.g. by the Government's own definition, it could be psychological, financial or emotional – none of which may involve actual physical violence but may involve aggression, cruelty, sadism or hostility (all various forms of 'violence').

In short, domestic violence is one person exerting systematic abusive power and control over another.

Domestic violence can be experienced by women and men whatever their age, ability, race, colour, class, religion or sexuality and the violence can begin at any stage of a relationship and may even continue after the relationship has ended.

It is usually women who are at the receiving end of domestic violence, and it is often men who are responsible. However, men are also victims of domestic violence from female partners.

It is also important to remember that domestic violence also exists within gay, lesbian, bi-sexual and transgender relationships.

7.1 Domestic Violence Against Women

In the UK, police receive a call from the public for assistance for domestic violence every minute of every day. This leads to police receiving an estimated 1,300 calls each day or over 570,000 each year[21]. However, according to a report based on the British Crime Survey, only 40.2% of actual domestic violence crime is reported to the police[22].

The statistics on violence against women in the UK make grim reading;

- It is estimated that every 20 seconds a woman in the UK is hit by her partner.[23]
- 1 in every 3 women will suffer from domestic violence at some point in their lives.[24]
- 1 in 8 women are repeatedly assaulted by their partner.[25]
- On average a woman is assaulted 35 times before reporting it to the police.[26]
- The psychological effects of domestic violence can include depression, anxiety, post traumatic stress disorder, flashbacks, nightmares, exaggerated startle response and suicide attempts.[27]
- 3 in 10 women using health services have been hurt by someone they know or live with.[28]

---

[21] Stanko, 2000
[22] Dodd et al, July 2004
[23] Home Office, Crime in England and Wales, 2006/07
[24] Home Office, Crime in England and Wales 2006/07
[25] British Crime Survey, 1996
[26] British Crime Survey, 1996
[27] James-Hanman, 1999
[28] British Medical Association, 2007

- Almost a third of domestic violence starts during pregnancy and existing violence often escalates during it.[29]
- Every 3 days a woman in the UK dies due to injuries received from their violent partner. [30]

But domestic violence against women is not unique to the UK. It occurs in virtually every community, every culture and every country across the world.

It is so prolific that the United Nations General Assembly has designated the 25th November as the '*International Day for the Elimination of Violence against Women*' and has asked for Governments, relevant agencies, bodies, and other international organisations and non-governmental organisations, to organise activities on the 25th November designed to raise public awareness of the problem of violence against women.

Many studies have been conducted into violence against women and some have tried to make sense of the male's actions citing alcoholism, stress from work, depression, peer pressure, retirement and unemployment as factors to blame for instigating the violence however it would appear that in almost 50% of these cases the women described the violence as their partner's 'normal behaviour'.

For help, advice or further information regarding Domestic Violence Against Women, see the 'Resources' section of this book.

7.2 Domestic Violence Against Men

It is now readily recognised that 1 in 3 women will become a victim of domestic violence at some point in their lives but do men also suffer domestic violence? It would seem they do – but this statistic tends to be neglected for two main reasons;

1) Males who are victims of domestic violence often see this as a slur on their manhood. A case of "It would be bad enough to be beaten up by a man but to be beaten up by a woman" – well, very few men would admit to that happening. And this is the crux of the problem. Men can be so engrossed in being macho that they are reluctant to come forward and report domestic violence to police, welfare officials, etc.

2) Males who are the perpetrators of domestic violence often use being the victim themselves as an excuse. A case of "She hit me first so I hit her back". This makes dealing with actual male victims much more difficult and on the few occasions when the police are called, it is the male victims, as opposed to the female perpetrators, that are usually arrested.[31]

In 2007, the British Medical Association revealed that 2 out of 10 men have been victims of domestic violence and 29% of men in gay relationships have been a victim of domestic violence at some stage in their lives. But as far back as the 1996 Scottish Crime Survey, 4% of men living in Scotland have reported regular violence or threats from their partners or ex-partners.

Initially, you would expect to hear that the cases of Scottish women reporting violence or threats would be much greater when compared to men, but there is only a small difference: 6% of women compared to 4% of men.

Resources for information on violence against men can be found, although they are admittedly not as abundant as those for violence against women (see 'Resources' section for details).

---

[29] Why Mothers Die, op cit, 2005
[30] Home Office, Crime in England & Wales 2006/7
[31] Stitt and Macklin, 1995

Most of these studies listed in the 'Resources' section have looked at male victims of female-on-male abuse and listed similarities in the range of degradation by the female partners of the men including flirting with other men, ridiculing the man's sexual potency in front of others (including their children), damaging the man's clothes, consistent threats to attack the man in their sleep, threats to harm children (both born and unborn), telling the police that self-inflicted injuries were caused by the man resulting in the man being wrongfully arrested and the threat of taking their children away from them.

Some of the men were even attacked by other men who had wrongly been informed that the woman involved was the victim.

The scope of physical violence endured by these men ranged from biting, scratching, punching, stabbing, having teeth knocked out, being scalded with boiling water, attacks to the genitalia and being beaten with home appliances and implements. Some of the men are still living with their abusive partners, in the majority of cases to protect their children.

Many of the men reported that their partners had consciously tried to injure them on the face and arms, making their injuries open to public scrutiny and the possibility of public humiliation and embarrassment. And in most of the cases, the abuse also involved sustained verbal, emotional and psychological forms of cruelty and, in common with female victims of domestic violence, many of the male victims stated that this form of emotional abuse together with the fear of violence was actually more devastating than the physical harm done, even on the occasions where this was extensive.

Some of these studies have tried to make sense of the female's actions citing alcoholism, childbirth, post-natal depression, PMS, eating disorders, retirement and unemployment as factors to blame for instigating the violence however in one study, 40% of the men interviewed described the violence as their partner's 'normal behaviour'.

For help, advice or further information regarding Domestic Violence Against Men, see the 'Resources' section of this book.

7.3 Domestic Violence Against Children

A study published by Cardiff University's Violence Research Group in August 2008 found that violence against babies and young children under 10 years old in England and Wales more than doubled from 2006 to 2007 (8,067 in 2007 compared with 3,805 in 2006).

In 2006, ChildLine counsellors spoke to nearly 50,000 children who had been affected by bullying or physical abuse.

In 2007, the charity National Society for the Prevention of Cruelty to Children (NSPCC) urged Gordon Brown to use his first 100 days as Prime Minister to help tackle violence against children because iIn any 100 day period, it is estimated that 205,000 children will witness domestic violence.[32]

Children are affected both mentally and/or physically by either seeing domestic violence being perpetrated between their parents or guardians or by being a direct victim of domestic violence themselves.

Tragically, it is estimated that one in six children in the UK will be sexually abused before their 16th birthday.[33]

Domestic Violence Against Children is a growing problem in the UK but it is a greater issue in other nations, especially the poorer countries.[34]

For help, advice or further information regarding Domestic Violence Against Children, see the 'Resources' section of this book.

---

[32] Women's Health: Into the Mainstream, Department of Health, 2002
[33] Child Maltreatment in the United Kingdom – a study of the prevalence of child abuse and neglect', NSPCC 2000.
[34] Beyond Individual War Trauma: Domestic Violence Against Children in Afghanistan and Sri Lanka, Catani, Schauer & Neuner, 2008

7.4 Domestic Violence Against the Elderly (Elder abuse)

The extent of abuse suffered by older people in the UK is detailed in a 2007 report released by Comic Relief and the Department of Health titled "**The UK Study of Abuse and Neglect**".

This report shows that 342,000 older people face abuse in their own homes within the UK with over 100,000 being physically assaulted and over 42,000 suffering sexual abuse. 227,000 elderly people in the UK were neglected or abused by family, close friends and care workers in the last year alone and the majority of the incidents involved a partner (51%) or another family member (49%).

In many cases elderly people are being left in bed, or unwashed, or left without food or access to the toilet.

While two thirds of abusers are family members, nearly one tenth are domiciliary care staff. (20% of theft is by domiciliary care staff.)

Commenting on the report, the Chief Executive of Action on Elder Abuse (AEA), Gary Fitzgerald, said; "The abuse of older people is a blight on our society and there is a duty on all of us to face up to the challenges posed by this Report. The four Governments of the UK must now begin to give the same level of priority to the abuse of adults as we see with children. At the end of the day, we hurt just as much at 78 years as we do at 8 years of age."

Woman's Aid also produced a report in 2007 titled "**Older women and domestic violence**". This report found that it is often assumed that domestic violence is mainly experienced by younger women and confirmed that there is no firm data about the extent of domestic violence against older women.

The report showed that older women experience even more barriers to disclosure than younger women and may therefore be more reluctant to report violence. There are also additional factors as to why it may be more difficult for an older women to disclose abuse, such as they feel that marriage is for life and they are ashamed, they are frightened that no one (including their adult children) will believe them or that they believe that it is too late at their age for them to seek help as services only exist for younger women.

In some instances, the abuse suffered by the elderly was instigated from their own adult children and included psychological and emotional attacks, physical violence and financial abuse e.g. as their pension was kept from them and personal banking accounts withdrawn without their knowledge.

Another hurdle with domestic violence with this age group is the understanding of exactly what is classed as domestic violence / domestic abuse. Domestic violence was not regarded as a crime when these victims were younger, and neither police action nor protection from the civil courts was readily available.

Commenting on this report, the Chief Executive of Women's Aid, Nicola Harwin CBE, said; "Health and social care professionals can impact on this situation by failing to respond to domestic violence experienced by older women or by responding inappropriately. This can include a failure to recognise either that the abuse is happening or to hold the abuser responsible - particularly if they are elderly or disabled. Health professionals should also not assume that any allegations of domestic violence by older women must be the result of confusion or dementia."

For help, advice or further information regarding Domestic Violence Against the Elderly, see the 'Resources' section of this book.

8. Personal Safety for Drivers

Never assume that simply because you are driving a vehicle that you are safe. You may want to take the following precautions;

In all road and weather conditions, check that your tyres have plenty of tread depth and are maintained at the correct pressure.

Always ensure that your vehicle is well preserved and serviced but remember that the weather can play havoc with your car and your driving ability so it is extremely important to regulate your personal car maintenance in time with the seasons.

In the summer months top up your windscreen washer bottles with a suitable windscreen detergent wash as this will help take off the copious amounts of flies you get on your windscreen. Water alone will not do this job adequately leaving streaks and poor visibility.

In the winter months keep your lights, windows and mirrors clean and free from ice and snow. Add anti-freeze to your car radiator and winter additive to the windscreen washer bottles.

If the weather is bad, use dipped headlights and reduce your speed and remember, in wet weather, stopping distances will be at least double but in icy conditions it can take ten times longer to stop your car than if on a dry road.[35]

If you must drive in poor conditions, make sure *you* are prepared and not just your car. Check the radio for local and national weather forecasts and travel information. Plan your journey in advance and ask yourself "Is this journey absolutely essential?"

Tell someone at your destination what time you expect to arrive and make sure you are equipped with warm clothes, food, boots and a torch and in snowy / blizzard conditions, take a spade to help dig your car wheels out of drifts.

If you break down on the motorway, wait outside your car preferably on the embankment as far away from the motorway as possible. Do not be tempted to cross the carriageway and don't accept (or for that matter, give lifts) to people you don't know.

You should find some signs directing you to the nearest emergency payphone. Most of these have CCTV cameras trained on them and can offer assistance in minutes if need be.

If you have a mobile phone, use it to relay your position to a recovery service or the police but never use a handheld mobile phone when you are driving.

8.1 Car Crime

And remember too that it is not just weather conditions that can cause you problems during the winter. From December through until March there is an abundance of shopping sales and plenty of shoppers around. Car parks are at their fullest and at this time of year, your car is likely to be packed with bargains, presents and luxury items which were on 'special offer'. An ideal time for the car thief!

Despite vehicle crime falling by over 37% in the last 10 years, there are still more than 2 million vehicle related thefts each year.

Here are a few facts relating to these thefts which you may find of interest:

- The UK is the car crime capital of Europe.[36]
- In the UK a car is stolen every minute.[37]
- In Britain, a stolen car is purchased every 20 minutes.[38]

---

[35] Home Health UK Ltd, 2007
[36] RAC Foundation, 2008
[37] Gap Insurance, 2008
[38] Trisign Vehicle Crime Awareness, 2010

- 40% of all cars stolen in the UK are never returned to their owners.[39]
- Over half a million cars are stolen in the UK each year.[40]
- Over 30% of vehicle crime occurs in car parks.[41]
- Vehicles left in public car parks are 200 times more likely to be stolen or abused than those garaged at home.[42]
- Over 80% of people are emotionally affected when their vehicle is broken into or stolen.[43]

Your car may seem safe to you if you live in a small town or village compared with the big cities but the days of leaving your car door unlocked are long gone. Opportunist thieves may find your unlocked car too big a temptation to resist.

Visit any small town in the UK and you will be amazed at how many drivers you will see jumping out of their car to pop into the Post Office or local shop whilst leaving their engine running. A 'quick visit' can last anything between 5 and 10 minutes – plenty of time for the opportunist thief to make off with your vehicle.

The usual response to this is; "Yes, but car thieves don't live in my area" and where that is no doubt true in our smaller, almost crime free areas, a factor we must take into consideration is that thieves are finding it harder and harder to steal in the big towns and cities (what with CCTV, patrolled car parks, etc.) and are heading to smaller towns and villages where some people still live by the old values and leave their cars unlocked.

Times are changing and if you don't change with them, you could live to regret it.

Here are some Golden Rules to avoid car crime happening to YOU:

- Always lock your car when you leave it and even while you're driving. If you feel unsafe driving with your doors locked (in case of accident) only unlock the doors when you are driving at speed – a criminal cannot get into your car if you are not stopped or driving very slowly.
- Keep the car windows rolled up especially when you're making slow progress in traffic. As with leaving the door unlocked, it only takes a few seconds at a stoplight for a thief to reach in and take whatever you've left on a seat.
- When you leave your car, always take the ignition key with you. Don't pop back into the house or into the Post Office leaving the engine running – your car may not be there when you come back out.
- At home, keep your car keys, including your spare set, safe and out of sight. Many people hang their car keys up near to the front door – a fact which many criminals know and look out for.
- Don't leave your belongings on display when you park your car. Don't leave papers lying around - especially private mail with your address on it or documents like vehicle registration or driving licence forms. Even your jacket or a plastic bag can tempt a 'smash and grab' thief.
- Get a car stereo you can remove and take with you. Mark it with your registration number or postcode using an ultra-violet pen and make a note of the serial number to keep in a safe place.

[39] Metropolitan Police, 2009
[40] Metropolitan Police, 2009
[41] Metropolitan Police, 2009
[42] Trisign Vehicle Crime Awareness, 2010
[43] Reducing Vehicle Crime, Home Office, 2005

- Have your car registration number or the last 7 digits of your Vehicle Identification Number (VIN) etched onto all windows, both windscreens and your headlamps. Alternatively, have your car's registration number etched onto all glass surfaces. Some insurance companies offer this service free when you join them so look out for these deals.
- Use a steering wheel lock every time you leave your car. Don't be tempted to buy the handbrake locks. Although they are not as expensive as steering wheel locks, they can be easily disregarded by a would-be thief simply by unscrewing the top of the gear stick. The entire locking devise can then be slipped off the gear stick leaving your car free to be driven away.
- Get a lockable petrol cap. Most new cars have these as standard but check it out if you're buying.
- Locking wheel nuts are cheap, easy to buy, easy to fit and very difficult to get off without a key. They simply stop thieves from taking your wheels so if you're buying, look out for these as standard on new cars.
- If you haven't got an immobiliser and you value your car, seriously think about getting one. An electronic engine immobiliser will prevent your car from starting and is the best way to stop thieves in their tracks. All immobilisers should be professionally fitted by an approved dealer - you can find one through the Vehicle Systems Installation Board.
- If you're buying a very special / expensive car, it may already have a tracking device installed or your insurance company may want you to fit one. It's worth finding out.
- Car alarms can deter thieves from not only stealing your car but also from taking items from inside it. All car alarms should be fitted by a professional installer – you can find one through the Vehicle Systems Installation Board.
- If you have a garage, use it. Straight away you have decreased your chances of having your car stolen by 40%. Remember to always lock both your car and your garage – you don't want to make things too easy for a thief.
- If you don't have a garage, always try to park in a well-lit, open place. A thief will not want people to see him breaking into your car and so will pick the vehicles which are parked in dimly lit areas.
- When parking outside always try and park your car in an attended car park. If this cannot be done, try to look for a public car park which is part of the police approved 'Secured Car Parks Scheme'. Do you know where your nearest secured car park is located?

How many of these tips you choose to adopt depends on a variety of things - the value of your car, how much *you* value your car, how much you value the people driving your car, etc. One things for sure though - it does not depend on where you live. Car crime can happen just as easily to a resident in a sleepy village as it can to a resident in the big city.

One or two changes to your daily routine or a minor modification to your vehicle may be all that is necessary and will most definitely reduce your chances of being a victim of car crime.

8.2 Road Rage

Most drivers feel relatively safe in their vehicle but road rage is becoming far more commonplace and is already a more frequent occurrence than you might think;

- Nearly **9 in 10** UK drivers between the ages of 16yrs and 30yrs say they have been road rage victims at least once.
- **20%** have experienced road rage **more than 10 times**.
- More than **70%** admitted committing the offence themselves.
- Road rage in the UK can be broken down into various regions:
  - 29% victims in South East of England
  - 18% in North of England
  - 15% in Eastern England
  - 6% in Scotland
  - 5% in Wales
  - 3% in Northern Ireland
- The most common action was gesticulating, while in 1 in 7 cases victims faced an aggressor who got out of the car and physically or verbally abused them. Only 7% reported incidents to the police.
- The most common location for road rage is in a town (54%), followed by a major A road (17%) or a motorway (15%).[44]

If you are verbally abused by another driver in an incident of road rage, drive off. Do not get involved in a tit-for-tat argument or resort to insulting hand signals as this can easily escalate the situation.

Be aware of the 'Warning Signs' and 'Danger Signs' the person is displaying and get ready to defend yourself if need be. If your current self defence instructor does not cover defending yourself while in a driving position – ask them why not.

8.3 Carjacking

Over the past few decades we have seen a steady rise in the number of carjacking incidents across the world and in the UK over the past decade. Some of these incidents have involved carjackers brandishing firearms, some brandishing knives and some brandishing syringes allegedly full of AIDS contaminated blood.

Before finding out how to prevent carjacks happening to you, let's see why they occur in the first place;

Carjacking has probably been around since the invention of the motor vehicle but the number of actual cases have been so minute that it passed by relatively unnoticed until the mid 1980s.

The concept of stealing a vehicle, without activating any alarms or cutting through steering wheel lock devices, driving off with it relatively undamaged and the bonus of having the original vehicle keys was jumped on by car thieves around the world.[45] Some carjackers are more sophisticated than others though. While working in South Africa as a Close Protection Officer (Bodyguard), I heard of the 'Amateur' and 'Professional' Carjackers;

- The 'Professional' Carjacker will see a car stopped at a red light and approach the driver's side from behind (usually at a 45 degree angle - the driver's 'blind spot'). The first thing the driver notices is a tap on his door window and he will see a person pointing a gun at him asking him politely to get out of the car. When he gets out, the carjacker simply gets in and drives off leaving him stranded.

---

[44] Driver Survey by Max Power, 2008
[45] Jacobs, Topalli & Wright, 2003

- The 'Amateur' Carjacker will do the same but will not risk a confrontation with the driver and so he will point the gun at the driver and, without warning or provocation, shoot him / her. The carjacker will then drag the driver's body out of the car and drive off in the blood splattered car which now has a smashed window - sure, he won't get as much money for it but he will get more than enough to pay for the bullet he just used. The other 'bonus' for the 'Amateur Carjacker' is that any vehicles behind his unfortunate victim will no doubt stop to offer First Aid rather than chase after the carjacker.

In South Africa where carjackings have been recorded since 1976, they reached their peak in 2001/02 with some 15,846 carjackings taking place. By 2003/04 these figures dropped slightly to 13,793.[46] In the USA it is estimated that some 49,000 carjackings and attempted carjackings occur each year.[47] This crime wave has now reached the UK and is on the increase daily.

Vehicle robbery including carjacking (but also theft of keys from bags and coats) comprised four percent of UK key thefts in 2001[48]. Analysis of these figures reveal that approximately one percent of all vehicle thefts in the United Kingdom were the result of carjacking – and with more than 1.1 million vehicles stolen in England and Wales alone between 1998 and 2001, that's a lot of carjackings!

Similar to South Africa, the UK also has different types of carjacker;

The 'Professional' Carjacker targets high priced cars to order (Porsche, Ferrari, etc.) with the buyers usually based overseas.[49]

The 'Semi-professional' Carjacker steals executive-type cars where the buyers are usually based in the UK and the car is simply re-sprayed or even just re-number plated.

The 'Opportunist thief / Joyrider' steals any fast driving car with no thought of passing it on. He may get a buyer for the buyer or he may just sell the CD player or he may simply trash the car.

So, where does carjacking occur? Well, the answer is obviously "anywhere" but statistics show that it usually occurs in the larger cities and most often in locations such as car parks, shopping centres, petrol stations, busy junctions where the driver has to stop and road traffic lights where the driver has to stop.

It also usually occurs when the owner is entering or exiting the vehicle and most carjackings or attempts (63% according to a study by the USA's Department of Justice National Crime Victimisation Survey 2007) occur within five miles of the victim's home or work place.

Remember, carjackers have to get you to stop or slow down to get your car and so they have devised ways to get you to stop. The two most successful in both the States and in South Africa are the 'Bump' and the 'Fallen Number Plate' – both of which have been successfully tried by UK carjackers.

'The Bump' is where the carjacker will intentionally bump your vehicle from behind, usually only lightly and at low speed to avoid any great damage. Inevitably, the victim will pull over, stop and get out to exchange insurance details. The carjacker's accomplice (who is usually the carjacker's passenger) will then make off with your vehicle and the carjacker will also speed off leaving you stranded by the road side.

'The Fallen Number Plate' is where the carjackers will see the type of vehicle they want (remember, sometimes these criminals are stealing to order) and follow it until it parks. They will then unscrew the back number plate and wait until the victim drives off again. At some point, usually near a quieter stretch of road, the carjacker and his accomplice will overtake the victim and toot their car horn to attract the victim's attention. The victim will

---

[46] Du Plessis & Louw, 2005
[47] US Department of Justice Bureau of Justice carjacking report 1992 – 1996
[48] Levesley et al, 2003
[49] Davis, 2003

then notice this nice person waving the number plate which must have fallen off their car at some point. Relieved to get their number plate back, the victim will inevitably pull over and get out to retrieve the plate from this 'Good Samaritan'. The carjacker's accomplice will then make off with your vehicle and the carjacker will drive off leaving you once again stranded by the road side.

What can YOU do to prevent this happening to you? Be aware of your surroundings and follow these simple steps:

- Always park in well-lit areas, if you know that it will be dark when you arrive / leave, don't park in an isolated or visually obstructed area (near walls, large hedgerows or at the far end of dimly lit multi-storey car park).
- As you walk to your vehicle, walk with purpose and stay alert. Watch for any suspicious persons sitting in cars or loitering around cars (perhaps looking nervous, handing out flyers, asking for directions, etc)
- If you are female, you may wish to ask for a security escort if you are alone at a shopping centre.
- As you approach your vehicle, have your vehicle keys in your hand. It helps you get into your vehicle faster and they can also be used as a weapon if you are attacked.
- As you get closer to your vehicle, look under, around, and inside. If safe, open the door, enter quickly, and lock the doors. Don't forget you can be an easy target if you are not alert and have your back turned while loading the boot or back seat up with shopping bags.
- Always drive with your vehicle doors locked - if you are not keen on this (in case you have an accident and emergency services cannot gain quick access to you) unlock your doors when you are driving at speed and lock them when driving around town or stopped.
- Always have your windows rolled up. If you don't have air conditioning, roll your window down but no more than a couple of inches.
- When stopped in traffic, leave room to manoeuvre and escape. As a rule of thumb, if you can see the entire back wheel of vehicle in front of you, you have enough room to manoeuvre out.
- Don't stop to assist a stranger whose vehicle has broken down. Assist instead by calling the Police to help.
- If you are bumped in traffic and the offending vehicle has more than just the driver, be suspicious of the accident. Memorise or jot down the vehicle's registration number and description. Wave the offending vehicle to follow and drive to the nearest Police Station or a busy place or a petrol station (as they all have floor court CCTV) before getting out.
- If you do get out of your vehicle, take your keys (and purse or wallet if you have one) with you and stay alert.
- If you are ever confronted by a carjacker, don't resist. It is better to live and claim back on the insurance than to risk death over a car.
- Never agree to be kidnapped. Drop the vehicle keys and run and scream for help. If you are forced to drive, consider crashing your vehicle in any busy area so passers-by can offer assistance and call the Police.
- Call the Police immediately to report the crime and try to remember a description of the carjackers and the vehicle they may have used.

If you remember nothing else, always remember that your vehicle has to be stationary or slowing to a stop to be carjacked. Carjackers cannot carjack your vehicle if it is moving.

With this in mind, when driving in urban areas keep a close watch on traffic lights. When lights show red, don't drive at your normal speed towards them, slow down and by the time you reach them they should be changing to green again.

Keep your car moving, stay vigilant when stopped and you won't be carjacked.

9. Personal Safety for Children

It is a well known fact that children and the elderly are the two most vulnerable groups in society. With that in mind, I would like to encourage children, parents and carers to check their knowledge, their behaviour and their surroundings - helping them take practical steps to prevent childhood accidents and improve their personal safety.[50]

9.1 Accidents

Accidents are a leading cause of death among children and young people. In the UK alone, according to the UK's National Society for the Prevention of Cruelty to Children (NSPCC), every year approximately *350* children will be killed in accidents and a further *2 million* will be rushed to hospital ER departments after an accident.

Some of the biggest hazards are falling down stairs (*33,000* children under fives each year in the UK), swallowing something harmful (*25,000* under fives each year in the UK), scald injuries from hot drinks (*9,100* under fives each year in the UK) and almost **200** children are killed in road accidents with *4,600* children seriously injured each year in the UK alone.

Accidents can be prevented by following some easy safety measures such as:

- Checking that your stairs are free from clutter to avoid trips and falls.
- Storing chemicals out of reach in childproof containers.
- Checking that your kettle has a short flex to prevent young children grabbing long, dangling kettle leads.
- Don't let your children play on or near roads.

Some dangers towards children are not however that apparent. Parents are becoming increasingly aware that a bigger danger looms on their children other than accidents and that is the threat of physical assault or abduction.

The number of children attacked or assaulted in the UK is steadily rising but what do we, as parents, guardians and teachers, do about it?

Many people ensure their children know how to cross the road properly using the old Green Cross Code system of looking left then right before attempting to cross.

Many people teach their children the difference between right and wrong, good manners and bad.

Some even go as far as teaching their children basic First Aid skills - but how many of us take the time to teach our child what to do if faced with a bully or how to defend themselves against an attacker?

What would happen if you, not your child, had an accident in the home? Would *your* child know what to do? Can they use the telephone? Who would they phone and would they know where to find their number? Do they know First Aid and could they open your airway until help arrives, for example? Is there a 'safe' house they can get help from? Is there a house you definitely would not want them to go to?

The following statistics revealed by the UK's Crimestoppers and the Home Office in 2007 paint a harrowing picture:

- *18%* of children in the UK are victims of assault. *51%* of these victims said they did not report the crimes to the Police and *45%* said they did not tell their parents.
- On average, *7 child murders* and *60 child abductions* occur annually in the UK.
- *73%* of children's deaths in the UK are caused by a family member or someone the child knows. Of the cases of child abuse in Scotland, *95%* of the victims knew their attacker.

---

[50] All statistics in this section are supplied by Kidscape (2007) and the Highland Wellbeing Alliance (2007) unless stated otherwise.

- **10%** of adults visiting their GP showed signs of sexual abuse. Of those, 40% were males, 60% were females.
- *Each year*, **10 - 14 child suicides** are directly attributed to bullying.
- **1 in 12 children** are badly bullied to the point that it effects their education, relationships and even their prospects for jobs later in life.

9.2 Bullies

Does your child know how to verbally fend off bullies?

If the bully got physical, can your child defend himself / herself?

Does your child know who to report a bully to?

9.3 Strangers

What does your child think a stranger looks like? Is it someone dressed in black with a cape or someone they just don't know? Is there a difference between a stranger in a uniform such a police officer or shopping assistant and a passer-by or customer?

Does your child know what to do if they are approached by a stranger?

Do they know who to report a stranger to?

If a stranger gets physical, can your child defend himself / herself?

9.4 Abusers

Does your child know the difference between a good touch (cuddles, hugs, kissing, stroking,) and a bad touch (punches, hitting, kicks, pushing) – and do they know who should be giving good touches and who should not?

Does your child know the difference between a good secret (the ones that make them feel good and happy) and a bad secret (the ones that make them feel sad and dejected)?

Does your child know not to keep secrets from you?

If someone they know gets physical or touches them inappropriately, can your child defend himself / herself?

9.5 Paedophiles

There are a lot of myths and misconceptions regarding paedophiles and hopefully this myth busting section will help clear things up;

- *Myth* - Paedophiles are always male.

Not true - They can be either male or female. In fact, the first person to be placed on the Sex Offenders list in Scotland was a female.

- *Myth* - Paedophiles are usually homosexuals.

Not true - 40% of paedophiles are homosexuals (less than half). Of those 40%, most had been sexually abused themselves as a child.

- *Myth* - Paedophiles are usually single and usually loners.

Not true - the profile of the average paedophile is a heterosexual, married man with children.

- *Myth* - Paedophiles are usually mentally ill.

Not true - Only 2% are mentally ill and need psychiatric help.

- *Myth* - My child is at more of a risk from a stranger than someone they know.

Not true - 66% of paedophiles are known to the child.

And the most chilling statistic of all..........
  • *Myth* - Paedophiles are caught and convicted fairly quickly.
Not true - The average paedophile, upon conviction, has conducted **275 offences** on **75 victims**.

And what about self defence? Can your child defend themselves against an attacker – be it another child or an adult?

As previously mentioned, always begin your defence by shouting "Get Back" aggressively and then, if there is no other escape, defend yourself. The same goes for children. A full blown kick to the shin by a child is extremely painful and may be enough to surprise the attacker into letting the child go.

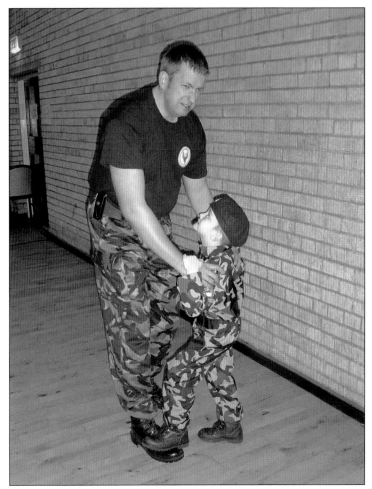

If not, a stamp to an attacker's foot may be more effective and remember a child may be just the right height to punch the attacker's groin or hit his face if the attacker bends over.

Children can even be taught basic strikes such as a right cross punch pictured above.

If grabbed and lifted up, children should be taught to scratch, pull hair, head butt, bite – anything and everything to break free.

Children have a surprising amount of determination as these photos show. This child was asked to push the 'attacker' on the face and he continued until our instructor's mask fell off.

You can see the determination in this child's face and how difficult it would be for an abductor to run off with him.

10. Personal Safety on the Internet

Log onto any internet social / conversation based forum such as Face Book, Bebo or YouTube and you will be surprised at the number of people who have entered their personal details such as their full name, address and/or date of birth. Don't be fooled into divulging this information. Use a nickname instead of your real name and leave it at that. If you need to give out a location, make it as broad as possible, for example, London instead of your exact address or district.

When shopping on-line, ensure the site you are using protects your personal details. All good shopping websites have secure transaction systems but make sure you look for a secure padlock symbol which shows adequate security software is in place to protect your information.

10.1 Children and the Internet

Learning about internet technology is part of the school National Curriculum in the UK. All schools have a policy on the teaching of Information and Communications Technology in classrooms and teachers will include the internet when teaching. Access to websites in this environment is strictly controlled and restrictions are applied to any site deemed 'unsuitable'.

It is also likely that your child has access to a computer at home and may use the internet to complete homework, build knowledge or simply to play games.

It is also worth bearing in mind that it is far more likely that your child will come into contact with a sex offender via their computer than on the street where you live! 80% of children access the internet alone. Over 22% have access in their bedrooms.[51]

There is no doubt that it is a lot harder to supervise your child's access to unsuitable web sites in your home than in the classroom. Here a few tips to help;

- Talk to your children about internet safety. Explain to them that there are people who will pretend to be younger than they are in order to meet up with you.
- Let them know that it's okay to inform you if they have a problem.
- Always keep the computer in the lounge or a family shared room.
- Encourage your children to be open about any friends they make over the internet. Remind them that the young person they are 'chatting' with on the computer may not be as young as they think.

---

[51] Kid Shield, 2010

- If your child wants to meet up with someone they met on the internet remind them that they are still strangers and advise them never to meet with their on-line friend alone.
- Prepare the meeting in advance and inform others of where you are meeting, when you are meeting and when you intend to return.
- Downloaded files may have spyware or viruses attached to them so ensure your computer has a suitable virus checker and anti-spy system before you start.
- Some social websites are un-moderated which means those visiting will have to check for unsuitable and/or offensive content themselves. Always ensure your child is visiting a moderated or hosted website.
- Watch out for websites which have adult only /over 18's warnings.
- Remember that viruses can be spread through e-mail attachments so only open e-mails from people you know and be especially careful of the attachments.

11. Personal Safety in the Workplace

The British Retail Consortium's Retail Crime survey 2007 showed that violence, abuse and threats against shopkeepers have soared with over half a million incidents recorded in a year.

The survey revealed that the number of cases of physical violence against shopkeepers in Great Britain had risen by 50%, while violent threats against people working in the retail trade had doubled.

In 2007, 34,743 people injured in violence were treated in Accident & Emergency departments in England and Wales alone[52] so perhaps it is not surprising that a survey was published in 2008 on behalf of the Healthcare Commission by the Royal College of Psychiatrists which revealed that two-thirds of nurses in wards for older people had been physically assaulted, with injury including fractures, dislocations and black eyes.

In 2008, the British Medical Association's report "**Violence in the workplace - The experience of doctors in Great Britain**" showed that a third of doctors had experienced violence or abuse in the workplace within the last year. Almost a third of these doctors who reported experiencing workplace violence, experienced physical violence or abuse.

These incidents ranged from being spat at, kicked, punched, bitten, slashed and stabbed. A third of doctors who reported experience of physical violence or abuse, received minor injuries as a result of the incident and 5% reported serious injuries.

Regardless of your profession, where you work, when you work or your surroundings, employers must protect their employees. Employers have a Common Law *"Duty of Care"* to others and are required to ensure *"so far as is reasonably practicable"*, the safety of people to whom the workplace has been made available (even those who are merely visiting the workplace e.g. contractors).

Furthermore, a contract of employment imposes an obligation upon the employer to provide *'trust and support'* to employees in the performance of their work.

But what has this to do with personal safety and self defence?

11.1 The Law

I have already detailed the various laws which cover self defence and the use of force but there are also laws which cover assault;

Section 39 of the Criminal Justice Act 1988 describes an assault as:

*"Any act committed intentionally or recklessly, which leads another person to **fear** personal violence. An assault becomes battery if force is applied without consent."*

So, for example, by sending a lone estate agent to a house viewing with a person who is known to shout aggressively at staff, may have that estate agent fearing personal violence – and even although that violence may not occur, the fact that the estate agent is in fear is technically enough to class it as an assault.

By knowingly placing their employee in this situation without a proper evaluation of the risk, hazard and likelihood of an assault occurring may prove to be an act of negligence on the employer's part.

In specific relation to the workplace, there are laws which the employer, as well as the employee must comply with:

Section 2 of the Health & Safety at Work etc Act 1974 states that an employer must provide:

"such information, instruction, training and supervision as is necessary to ensure, so far as is reasonably practicable, the health and safety at work of his employees".

---

[52] Violence & Society Research Group, Cardiff University 2009

It goes on to say that employers have a statutory duty regarding *"the provision and maintenance of a working environment for his employees that is, so far as is reasonably practicable, safe, without risks to health, and adequate as regards facilities and arrangements for their welfare at work. "*

Unfortunately, many employers read this Act and felt that to ensure the health and safety of their employees meant avoiding accidents and so they began to provide Health & Safety training for their staff or First Aid training but very few went as far as personal safety / self defence training.

By 1995 however, the law felt it was time they explained exactly what an accident was and the RIDDOR (Reporting of Injuries, Diseases and Dangerous Occurrences Regulations) 1995 Regulations included an additional definition of 'an accident', which is:

"An act of non-consensual physical violence done to a person at work."

This now made it perfectly clear to employers that 'an accident' can also be an act of violence.

The Health & Safety Executive has since defined violence at work as:

"Any incident in which a person is abused, threatened or assaulted in circumstances relating to their work".

So how do you evaluate the risk of an act of violence occurring in your workplace?

Well, an employer can take measures to reduce the risk of violence against employees by implementing:

- Risk assessments of employees' work and work environment.
- Individual assessments of patients/pupils in the case of hospitals, nursing homes, mental health establishments, home helps, schools, etc.
- Relevant staff training including communication skills, violence and aggression de-escalating techniques, basic self defence skills and in some cases control and restraint techniques.
- Physical measures such as alarms.
- Maintaining the correct staffing levels to ensure no 'lone working' occurs.
- Maintaining safety precautions of logging and checking meetings etc.

11.2 Risk Assessment

Having analysed and evaluated past incidents of violence in their workplace, employers then need to introduce the necessary changes to prevent them occurring again.

The Management of Health & Safety at Work Regulations 1992 (amended 1999) states:

"An employer must undertake a general examination of their work activity, record significant findings and proceed to follow risk assessment with appropriate preventative and protective measures and management arrangements."

In other words, an employer needs to be able to produce a risk assessment for all aspects of their employees' work and where a high risk of violent attack is predicted or where employees face danger or place themselves in a dangerous environment for example, nursing in Accident & Emergency or lone visits by estate agents or social workers, etc. then employers must provide preventative measures such as a specific Health & Safety policy that identifies the hazards, how they will be controlled (perhaps by safety devices and equipment such as personal attack alarms, or perhaps through specific personal safety / self defence training, etc.) and who will be responsible for their implementation.

To produce a risk assessment, you first need to identify the hazard. A hazard is described as: *"Something with the potential to cause harm"* which is an all-encompassing definition.

You then need to think about how likely it is that the particular hazard you have highlighted will occur and what would be the outcome if it did. So your risk assessment is therefore defined as follows;

$$Risk = Hazard + Likelihood + Outcome$$

If you then give each area a value from 1-3 you can establish how high a risk each incident is, for example;

The hazard of a chambermaid being attacked whilst working alone in guests' bedrooms will be higher (3) than if they cleaned the public areas in view of lots of people (1). The likelihood of this kind of attack occurring however may be very low (1) but it may have occurred before so it may score (2) or (3) depending on the circumstances. The outcome of an attack could be sexual or even death – either one rating (3). The risk assessment score for this particular chambermaid may therefore be as high as 9.

By then marking the level of risk as follows:

- Low Risk   1 – 3   Leave for now
- Medium Risk   4 – 6   Possibly provide training / safety procedures
                              / alarm systems in the near future.
- High Risk   7 – 9   Act now.

We can begin to assess whether we need to take precautions, what those precautions may be and when (and by whom) they will need to be introduced.

So in the case of our chambermaid, we may decide to issue them all with two-way radios and/or personal attack alarms and we may even introduce a policy of radioing every hour to confirm where they are and if everything is okay. You may even adopt a code word that confirms their safety rather than a conversation which can be wrongly confirmed under duress.

Always remember, *be Proactive – not Reactive*.

Different jobs create different risks of workplace violence, for example, we all realise that a police officer, prison guard, door steward or security staff may all experience a greater risk of violence however retail staff who need to comply with age restrictions (regarding the selling of knives, firearms, cigarettes, alcohol, cinema tickets, etc.), traffic wardens, ticket inspectors, Accident & Emergency staff, housing department personnel, etc, also evoke risks in relation to violence.

Ensure your workplace has completed a risk assessment of your job and your employer knows what the law expects of them.

11.3 Staff Training

The best risk management tool an employer can provide is training. Regardless of where your workplace is – a shop, a public house, a hospital, a prison, a hotel, public transport - staff need to be trained on how to prevent an act of violence happening to them.

Staff need to be;
1. Trained in how to communicate effectively with people.
2. Trained in how to deal with angry people.
3. Trained in what to do (and not to do) to prevent theft and deal with argumentative / aggressive people.

These three triggers, according to crime prevention statistics, are responsible for 70% of all incidents of violence at work.

Your staff training should therefore include a good knowledge of the signs of aggression in a person i.e. the Warning Signs and Danger Signs, as well as what makes people act aggressively;

- Lack of confidence,
- Frustration,
- Past emotions,
- Anxiety,
- Stress overload,
- Mental health problems,
- Alcohol / drug abuse, etc.

Or it could be that the person you are dealing with feels;

- Embarrassed,
- Mocked,
- Insulted,
- Demoralised,
- That they are not being taken seriously, etc.

Aggressive tendencies can also be exacerbated by the environment;

- It may be too hot,
- It may be too cold,
- It may be too noisy,
- It may be too bright,
- There may be too many people, etc.

Escalating factors which can turn an angry person into a violent person depend on your response: an aggressive response can produce an aggressive comeback and a defensive response can also challenge the person to escalate the situation.

Staff must be taught how to deal with incidents in a way that do not provoke a heated argument, does not increase frustration and at the same time does not see them lose face.

Simple defusing techniques can be split into three areas; **Calming, Reaching and Controlling.**

Calming

- *Active listening* – Nod, look sympathetic, say "uh-huh" or "yes", smile, look sympathetic yet maintain an air of professionalism.
- *Voice Control* – Do not raise your voice, avoid sarcastic or sneering tones, do not belittle them.
- *Body language* – No folding your arms, sudden arm movements, hands on hips or hands behind back. Maintain natural eye contact (no staring or glowering).
- *Personal space* – Ensure you don't inadvertently enter the other person's personal space i.e. if a stranger approached you, as soon as they got within 1.2 – 3 metres of you (depending on each individual, the environment, etc.), you would begin to feel uncomfortable. Your 'normal' personal space is between 0.5 – 1.2 metres whereas

your intimate space is between 0 – 0.5 metres. It is important to also bear in mind that aggressive people have a wider buffer zone and so stepping within 4 metres may actually be perceived by them as an invasion of their own personal space requiring a defensive reaction.

Remember, *behaviour breeds behaviour*. Your good behaviour will serve to calm them down whilst your bad behaviour will merely exacerbate the situation.

Reaching
You have a choice about whether to confront your aggressor or not. You may choose to ignore them but this has to be weighed up – would it diffuse the situation or make it worse?

You may decide to confront your aggressor when they have calmed down.

Ensure that you agree with the aggressor that there is a problem. Try to get them to sit down. Write down their name, address, problem, etc. and get them to confirm. This will help calm them and enable you to reach out to them and allow effective communication to begin.

Controlling
If you have to confront an aggressor, do it assertively, not aggressively. Acting angrily will only make things worse but acting assertively shows the aggressor that you are in charge and are willing to help. For example, "I can appreciate that you are upset and angry but if you continue to shout at me I will be forced to ask you to leave so I need you to calm down."

Offer a solution to maintain control of the situation. If the situation still seems to be aggressive, offer any solution as an excuse to get away. For example, "I am sure I can do that for you, I just need to let my supervisor know what we are going to do."

Do's & Don'ts

Do
- Assess the situation continuously - Look for exits, witnesses, danger signs.
- Be ready to defend yourself if need be – run over 'what if' scenarios in your mind.

Don't
- Scream and shout unless you see the Danger Signs and feel threatened or are in danger.
- Touch the aggressor unless you are defending yourself.

11.4 Physical Measures
There are many physical ways to reduce the risks of violence in the workplace including the issuing of personal attack alarms, protective clothing (stab proof vests to police / security personnel or Kevlar gloves for door stewards, etc.), panic alarms – both hidden and in view, alternative escape routes (another exit from your office), CCTV camera installations, time locked safes, safety glass partitions, etc.

11.5 Safety Precautions

When dealing with personal safety in the workplace you should consider the location of your workplace – are you in an isolated area? Can you easily summon help? If so, are there plans to do this and how easily is this done?

What about **coded calls**? If you are placing yourself into a one-on-one scenario where you are left alone with another person, you may want to use coded calls for example,

"Please check my next appointment in the *blue* file."

May mean: "I don't feel safe here. Call me in five minutes to ensure I am okay."

"Please check my next appointment in the *red* file."

May mean: "I am in trouble. Call the Police."

Does your place of work have emergency panic alarm buttons or do they issue personal attack alarms?

What is the procedure for removal of a threat in your workplace? What are the escape procedures should a violent incident erupt? Do you receive regular training in 'what if' scenarios?

Other safety precautions to consider:

- Who you are meeting?
- Do you have to go alone?
- How long will the meeting last?
- Is it possible to visit during daylight hours?
- What is the location you plan to visit like? (remote / difficult to get to / in a bad area)
- How are you getting there and back? (taking your own/company car or a taxi or a bus)
- Are there any records / reports available to you so that you may assess the person you are visiting before you go?
- Logging meetings (colleagues & the person you are visiting)
- Say who you are, why you are there and show your ID if you have one. (remember you are the visitor)
- Check who you are talking to.
- Do not enter the house at all, if appropriate, if the person you are planning to visit is not available.
- Wait to be invited in or at least ask if you can go in.
- Let them know how long your visit will take.
- Let them lead the way, if appropriate.
- Check as you go in how the front door locks.
- Take care with documents you may not want them to see.
- Study your surroundings and look for an exit.
- Ensure you can get out quickly if need be. Sit nearest the door.
- Ask for dogs to be put in another room.
- Try not to react to bad, dirty or smelly surroundings.
- Remain alert. Watch for changes in mood, movements or expressions.
- Do not spread your belongings around as you may need to leave in a hurry.
- If you feel at risk – leave as soon as possible. Have an excuse ready e.g. you need to get a form from the car / you forgot to take your documents form the office / etc.

- Checking meetings (colleagues / manager / friends)
- Do you have a mobile phone / pager / change for a call box to help you get in touch with someone if you need help?
- If you are prevented from leaving or threatened, stay calm and try to control the situation using voice and body language techniques.
- Do what you have to do to protect yourself.
- Confirmation of a happy ending.

There are also many other safety precautions you may wish to implement in your workplace;

11.6 Working away from the Office / in other people's homes

Aggressive behaviour can be caused by people feeling that there is an intrusion into their private lives. The potential for violence against you while working away from the office / in other people's homes may therefore depend on why you are there or perhaps the person has had a bad experience with a previous colleague or caller or perhaps the person may simply be having a 'bad day'.

Logging meetings

Call as your meeting is about to start:

"Hi ...., I'm just meeting ...... at .... I should be finished at ..... Give me a call if I'm running late."

Trust your instincts – If you feel uncomfortable, make your excuses and leave. Arrange another meeting at another time in the company of another colleague.

It is better to be safe than sorry.

In 1986, a 25 year old estate agent named Suzy Lamplugh disappeared after she went to meet a man called Mr Kipper who had telephoned to book an appointment to view a house in Fulham, England. Her colleagues became suspicious when Suzy did not return from this 12.45pm appointment and she had missed a meeting with another client at 6pm. She was never seen again and has since been presumed murdered and officially declared dead in 1994.

Checking meetings

This is where the workplace calls just after your arranged meeting starts. The call can be used:

- To confirm everything is okay.
- As an excuse for you to leave an uncomfortable situation.
- To alert your workplace that something is wrong.

Confirmation

This is where you call your workplace to confirm that the meeting went as planned and that you are safely on your way to the next meeting / back to the Office / heading home.

11.7 Management Prosecution

Failure of a business or organisation to provide adequate controls and proper, safe working practices can now result in *management prosecution* under gross negligence should a serious injury or fatality occur at work.

In 2002, a personal injury claim, Cook v Bradford Community Health NHS Trust[53], saw a healthcare assistant being awarded compensation after being assaulted by a patient.

Ms. Cook worked as a healthcare assistant at a psychiatric hospital and as she was delivering cups of coffee to her colleagues in the 'seclusion suite' of a unit for violent patients, a patient asked to go to the toilet.

The patient was known by the hospital to be unstable, unpredictable and dangerous and while Ms. Cook was in the suite, the door was opened allowing him to get out.

He attacked Ms. Cook and as a result she suffered minor physical and severe psychiatric injuries.

The Court of Appeal said the defendants had a duty *"not to place her unnecessarily in a position where there is a risk of foreseeable danger"*. The risk could have been avoided by not having the patient out of his room.

If *gross negligence* is proven in a case, it can be classed as *management failure* and management can be prosecuted under this legislation for failing in their duty of care under the Health & Safety at Work Act 1974.

In 2002, a care worker, Elizabeth Barrett[54], was beaten un-conscious by a schizophrenic who threatened to kill her. She was punched to the floor by the male patient after she had volunteered to take him on a caravan holiday in Cumbria. Her colleague, Mellissa Darby, was also elbowed in the face as she tried to restrain the man.

Mersey Care NHS Trust was found guilty of breaching the Health and Safety at Work Act 1974 because it failed to carry out sufficient procedural checks. It was ordered to pay a substantial fine.

It is also prudent to bear in mind that if it can be proven that a business or organisation has no current safe systems of work, including personal safety training, currently in place and supported by policy, areas such as public and employer liability insurance may be void.

---

[53] Cook v Bradford Community Health NHS Trust, CA, 23 October 2002 [2002] EWCA Civ 1616
[54] R v Merseycare NHS Trust,Ormskirk MC, 5 September 2002

12. Final Word

It is a dangerous world out there and every area, every city, every life has its share of violence, abuse and neglect.

It is good to remember however that the chances of a violent attack happening to you in the UK are still quite small – so please don't have nightmares.

I hope that this book helps you, the reader, be aware of Personal Safety in all its forms and provides you with a complete understanding which allows you to take precautions and preventative measures to ensure that you don't become a victim.

Stay safe.

Alan Bell

Alan Bell
Founder & Principal Instructor of 'Security And Safety'

www.securityandsafety.co.uk

email: enquiries@securityandsafety.co.uk

13. Acknowledgments

Thanks to Paul Mogford of Apex News Pix for kindly permitting the use of the SWNS and APEX photos in the "Sexual Attack" section of this book.

Special thanks to my colleagues, friends and family who have helped with photographs for this book especially my niece, Tayler Amy-Louise Michaels, and my nephew, Josh Ryan Bell.

Additionally a big thank you to my brother, David Bell, who is a qualified personal safety / self defence instructor in his own right and without whom, many of the photographs would not be included in this book.

The biggest thanks of all though must go to my wife, Frances Bell, who has supported and encouraged me over the three years it took to research and complete this body of work and given me the time to put my thoughts into words.

This book is dedicated to my son, Daniel Aidan Bell and my newborn daughter, Gemma Rose Bell – you have both given me so much, I hope this book gives something to you.

Appendix A

REASONABLE FORCE QUIZ

Self Defence - What is Reasonable?

In the following incidents, a degree of force has been used by the victim. For each incident, think about the following:

a. Do you think it was "Reasonable Force"?
b. Should the victim be charged with any criminal offence?

1. You are passing a cash point when you see a young person punch an elderly person to the ground before grabbing, and running off with their cash. Your friend goes to help the injured person whilst you run after the offender, catch them and take hold of him with the intention of handing him over to the police. The offender hits you so you strike him back and when he falls to the ground you sit on him to prevent his escape.

2. Two young men are walking home from a football match when they are met and intimidated by four fans from the rival team. The four fans spit at the two young men and trip one of them up. The other young man is angry at this and lashes out to defend his friend. He uses his fists to punch one of the fans but is soon set upon by all four fans.

His friend who had been tripped up sees a broken house brick on the ground and uses it to strike at one of the fans causing a fracturing skull.

3. At 11a.m. a woman hears a knock at her door. She opens it and a middle-aged man puts his foot in the doorway and says that he has come to read the electricity meter. As she tries to shut the door, he forces his way into the house.

The woman screams in fear. Her 6-week-old baby is asleep in the lounge and she now fears for their safety.

The man drags her into the kitchen and begins to sexually assault her. She reaches for a bread knife and plunges it into the man's back. The man slumps to the floor and dies from blood loss on his way to hospital.

4. A barman has to physically eject a drunk from his pub. Whilst getting rid of the drunk, he trips over a stair and falls with the drunk. The drunk receives a cut to his face that requires stitching.

5. A 9-year-old boy is punched in the face by another boy in his class at school. The attack was completely unprovoked and the boy received a black eye.

His 14-year-old brother waits for his brother's attacker the next day and punches the younger boy in the face giving him a black eye.

***

Answer to Q.1: This would be considered as 'Reasonable Force'. You have used minimum force to restrain the offender after he has hit you.

Answer to Q.2: This would have been 'Reasonable Force' if the 'friend' had just used his fists to assist in defending himself and his mate. However, as soon as he started to use the 'brick' his actions could be deemed as 'Unreasonable' but the Court would weigh up the situation and perhaps allow this giving that their was four against two and they were being overpowered.

Answer to Q.3: There is no right and wrong answer to this question should this occur in real life the woman would almost certainly be arrested for 'Murder' and released on bail possibly pending the findings of a Coroner's inquest.

A jury would undoubtedly deliver a verdict of 'Not Guilty' as the man was not known to the woman and had entered her house unlawfully. Forensic evidence would also play a major part in her defence and provide proof of a sexual attack. Under these circumstances the Judge may wait for a Coroner's verdict before passing judgement.

The Coroner's inquest can decide if the death of the man was either Lawful in the circumstances (a verdict of 'Justifiable Homicide') or was Unlawful (a verdict of either Murder or Manslaughter).

Answer to Q.4: This would be classed as 'an accident'.

Answer to Q.5: The initial assault by the class member on the boy was 'Unlawful' but due to the age of the two boys (9 years), the offender is under the age of criminal responsibility (10 years) according to UK Law.

The assault by the 14-year-old boy on the 9 year-old is an Offence and is an 'Unreasonable Use of Force'.

The 14-year-old could be arrested and charged with the assault.

****

14. References

British Crime Survey 2009 parliamentary update, SN/SG/2617, Research Development and Statistics Directorate, London: Home Office via Gavin Berman & Gavin Thompson.

British Crime Survey 2008, SN 6066, Research Development and Statistics Directorate, London: Home Office.

British Crime Survey 2000, SN 4463, Research Development and Statistics Directorate, London: Home Office.

British Crime Survey 1996, SN 3832, Research Development and Statistics Directorate, London: Home Office.

Her Majesty's Inspectorate of Constabulary & Her Majesty's Crown Prosecution Service Inspectorate (January 2007), *'Without Consent'*, London: Home Office.

Home Office Development & Practice Report 21 (March 2004), *Crimes Against Students; Emerging Lessons for Reducing Student Victimisation.*

NSPCC & Sugar survey (March 2005), *Teen Abuse Survey of Great Britain.*

Trade Union Congress (January 1999), *Violent Times.*

European NEXT Study (March 2008), *Violence Risks in Nursing.*

Stanko (2000), *The Day to Count*, The National Domestic Violence Snapshot, Elizabeth Stanko, September 2000 (Stanko *"Enough is Enough"* Conference, October 2000, Women's Aid Newsletter, December 2000).

Dodd, T., Nicholas, S., Povey, D and Walker, A (2004), *Crime in England and Wales 2003/2004*. Home Office: London.

Kershaw, C., Nicholas, S and Walker, A (2007), *Crime in England and Wales 2006/2007*. Home Office: London.

Kershaw, C., Budd, T., Kinshott, G., Mattinson, J., Mayhew, P. and Myhill, A. (2000) *The 2000 British Crime Survey England & Wales*, Statistical Bulletins 18/00, Home Office Research, Development & Statistics Directorate: London.

Scottish Government (2008): *Lessons for Mental Health Care in Scotland.*

Ramonet I. (July 2004), *Violence Begins at Home*, Le monde Diplomatique (English edition).

James-Hanman, D (1999) 'Inter-Agency Work with Children and Young People' in Harwin, N, Hague, G and Malos, E (eds) *The Multi-Agency Approach to Domestic Violence. New Opportunities, Old Challenges?*

Lewis, Gwynneth, and Drife, James (2005) *Why Mothers Die 2000-2002: Report on confidential enquiries into maternal deaths in the United Kingdom (CEMACH).*

British Medical Association (2008), *"Violence in the workplace - The experience of doctors in Great Britain".*

Stitt and Macklin (1995), *'Battered Husbands': The Hidden Victims of Domestic Violence.*

Jacobs, Bruce A; Topalli, Volkan; Wright, Richard. (1st October 2003), *Carjacking, Streetlife and Offender Motivation*, British Journal of Criminology, Volume 43, Number 4, Oxford University Press.

US Department of Justice Bureau of Justice (2008), *Carjacking report 1992 – 1996.*

Levesley, T., Braun, G., Wilkinson, M. and Powell, C. (2003), *Emerging Methods of Car Theft – Theft of Keys,* Research Findings 239, London: *Home Office.*

Davis L. (1st August 2003), *Carjacking – Insights from South Africa to a New Crime Problem*, Australian and New Zealand Journal of Criminology, Volume 36, Number 2, Australian Academic Press.

UK Department of Health (2002), *'Women's Health: Into the Mainstream'.*

NSPCC (2000), *'Child Maltreatment in the United Kingdom – a study of the prevalence of child abuse and neglect'.*

Home Office (2005), *Reducing Vehicle Crime*, National Audit Office, HC 183 Session 2004-05.

Comic Relief & the UK Department of Health (2007), *"The UK Study of Abuse and Neglect".*

Women's Aid (2007), *"Older women and domestic violence".*

House of Commons Library (2007), *Rape Convictions as a Proportion of Recorded Rape Offence.*

Catani, Schauer & Neuner (2008), *"Beyond Individual War Trauma: Domestic Violence Against Children in Afghanistan and Sri Lanka".*

British Retail Consortium (2007), *Retail Crime Survey.*

Schaller, Bruce (April 1992), *Who's Driving New York?*, NYC Taxi and Limousine Commission.

Du Plessis, Anton; Louw, Antoinette (2005), *The Tide is Turning: The 2003/04 South African Police Service crime statistics*, SA Crime Quarterly No. 12, June 2005.

British Medical Association (2007), *"Violence in the Workplace - The Experience of Doctors in Great Britain".*

Healthcare Commission (February 2008); *National Audit of Violence in Mental Health Services*, Royal College of Psychiatrists.

Metropolitan Police (2007), *Project Sapphire.*

V Sivarajasingam, S Moore, JP Shepherd (2007), *Violence in England and Wales: An Accident and Emergency Perspective*, Violence and Society Research Group, Cardiff University.

Abrahams, C. (1994), *The Hidden Victims: Children and Domestic Violence*, London: NCH Action for Children.

Cook v Bradford Community Health NHS Trust, CA, (23 October 2002), EWCA Civ 1616.

R v Merseycare NHS Trust, Ormskirk MC, (5 September 2002).

Max Power (2008), *Driver Survey.*

Rape Crisis, Intervention & Prevention statistics obtained in November 2008 from www.rapecrisis.org/rape_facts

Statistics regarding *Date Rapes* in the UK obtained in November 2008 from Home Health UK Ltd at http://www.homehealth-uk.com/medical/daterape.htm

Scottish Lord Advocate, Elish Angiolini (2008), speech at the '*Rape Crisis Scotland*' conference.

Statistics regarding *Car Crime* in the UK obtained in November 2008 from;
Gap Insurance at www.motoworld.co.uk/gapinsurance
The RAC Foundation Car Crime Fact File at
www.racfoundation.org/index.php?option=com_content&task=view&id=87&Itemid=35
Metropolitan Police at www.met.police.uk/crimeprevention/vehicle
And from Trisign Vehicle Crime Awareness at /www.trisign.co.uk/vehicle_crime obtained in January 2010.

The Vehicle Systems Installation Board is the UK's national regulatory and accreditation body for installers of vehicle security and other electronic systems and is supported by: The Home Office, Motor Insurers & 'Thatcham', Security Manufacturers, Vehicle Manufacturers, Vehicle Retailers, Motor Organisations and many others. They can be found at www.vsib.co.uk

Statistics regarding *Personal Safety for Children* were obtained from 2007 - 2010 from the Home Office, Kidscape, Crimestoppers and the Highland Wellbeing Alliance.

Statistics regarding *Personal Safety on the Internet* obtained in January 2010 from 'Kid Shield'.

Section 3 (1) of the Criminal Law Act 1967.

Section 39 of the Criminal Justice Act 1988.

Section 2 of the Health & Safety at Work etc Act 1974.

Sexual Offences Act 2003.

RIDDOR (Reporting of Injuries, Diseases and Dangerous Occurrences Regulations) 1995 Regulations.

The Management of Health & Safety at Work Regulations 1992 (amended 1999).

The Health & Safety Executive's definition of Violence at Work, 2006.

"Get Tough – How to Win in Hand-to-Hand Fighting" by Major W.E. Fairburn.

"Kill or Get Killed" by Colonel Rex Applegate.

15. Resources

Statistical Bulletin Crime and Justice Series: Recorded Crime in Scotland 2007/08, ISBN 9780755972319A, National Statistics Publication for the Scottish Government.

Statistical Bulletin Crime and Justice Series: Recorded Crime in Scotland 2004/05, ISBN 0755927826, Scottish Executive National Statistics Publication, Scottish Government.

Statistical Bulletin Crime and Justice Series: Recorded Crime in Scotland 2003, ISBN 0755937503, Scottish Executive National Statistics Publication, Scottish Government.

Statistical Bulletin Crime and Justice Series: Recorded Crime in Scotland 2001, ISBN 0755933605, Scottish Executive National Statistics Publication, Scottish Government.

Mirrlees-Black, Catriona (1999), *Domestic Violence: Findings from a new British Crime Survey self-completion questionnaire*, Home Office Research Study 191, Research Development and Statistics Directorate Report, London: Home Office.

European Sourcebook of Crime and Criminal Justice Statistics (December 2003), 2nd edition published by the Dutch WODC (Scientific Investigative and Documentation Centre), publications series (nr. 212).

For help, advice or further information regarding *Domestic Violence Against Women*, contact Women's Aid at www.womensaid.org.uk or Refuge at www.refuge.org.uk or the Women & Equality Unit at www.womenandequalityunit.gov.uk/domestic_violence/index

For further information regarding the '*International Day for the Elimination of Violence against Women*' read; Council of Europe (2002), Recommendation Rec (2002)5 of the Committee of Ministers to Member States on the *Protection of Women Against Violence* and Explanatory Memorandum Adopted on 30 April 2002. (Strasbourg, France: Council of Europe) or visit www.un.org/depts/dhl/violence/index

Reports and studies referring to Domestic Violence Against Men include;

Gadd, David; Farrall, Stephen; Dallimore, Damian & Lombard, Nancy (September 2004), *Domestic Abuse Against Men In Scotland,* Scottish Executive Central Research Unit 2002, Dept of Criminology, Keele University

Phillip W. Cook (1997), *Abused Men.*

HM Inspectorate of Constabulary (1997), *Hitting Home.*

Brogden & Harkin (2000), *Male Victims of Domestic Violence,* Northern Ireland Domestic Violence Forum.

Tjaden and Thoennes (2000), *The* US *National Violence Against Women Survey.*

Henderson (2000), *The Scottish Partnership on Domestic Abuse*, Scottish Executive.

Lewis and Sarantakos (2001), *Abused Men In Australia and New Zealand.*

Scottish Executive (2000 & 2001), *Domestic Abuse Recorded by the Police.*

Gondolf, E. (1988) "Letters 'Continued Debate': *The Truth about Domestic Violence*", Social Work.

Hammerton, J. A. (1992) *Cruelty and Companionship: Conflict in Nineteenth-Century Married Life.*

Straus, M. (1993) *"Physical Assaults by Wives: A Major Social Problem"* in R. Gelles & D.R. Loseke (eds), *Current Controversies on Family Violence*, Sage: London.

Newburn, T. & Stanko, E. A. (1994) *"When men are victims: the failure of victimology"*, in T. Newburn & E.A. Stanko (eds) *Just Boys Doing Business? Men, Masculinities and Crime,* Routledge: London.

Cook, P. W. (1997) *Abused Men: the Hidden Side of Domestic Violence*, Praeger: London.

Hearn, J (1998) *The Violences of Men. How Men Talk About and How Agencies Respond to Men's Violence to Women*, London: Sage.

Wolf-Light, P. (1999) *"Men, violence and love"*, in J. Wild (ed) *Working with Men for Change*, UCL Press: London.

Mirrlees-Black, C. (1999) *Domestic Violence: Findings from a new British Crime Survey self-completion questionnaire*, Home Office Research Study 91, Home Office: London.

Flood, M. (1999) *"Claims about Husband Battering"* DVIRC Newsletter (August) 3-8, http://www.anu.edu.au/~a112465/XY/husbandbattering.htm

Soothill, K., Francis, B., Ackerley, E. & Collett, S. (1999) *Homicide in Britain: A Comparative Study of Rates in Scotland and England & Wales*, Scottish Executive Central Research Unit: Edinburgh.

Brogden, M. & Harkin, S. (2000) *Male Victims of Domestic Violence: Report to the Northern Ireland Domestic Violence Forum*, Institute of Criminology, Queen's University, Belfast.

Gadd, D. (2000) *"Masculinities, Violence, & Defended Psychosocial Subjects"* Theoretical Criminology, 4 (4): 429-50.

Rennison, C.M. & Welchans, S. (2000) *"Intimate Partner Violence"*, Bureau of Justice Statistics: Special Report, NCJ 178247: U.S. Department of Justice.

Morrison, C. & Mackay, A. (2000) *The Experience of Violence & Harassment of Gay Men in the City of Edinburgh*, Scottish Executive Central Research Unit: Edinburgh.

Rome, D. (2001) *"The Battle for Men's Rights in Scotland"*, www.angryharry.com

George, M. (2001) *"The Great Taboo"* Paper presented at conference *"Unlikely Victims"*, Pride Park Stadium, Derby 04 December 2001.
MacPherson, S. (2002) *Domestic Violence: Findings from the 2000 Scottish Crime Survey*, Scottish Executive: Edinburgh.

For help, advice or further information regarding *Domestic Violence Against Men*, contact the Men's Advice Line at www.mensadviceline.org.uk or Respect at www.respect.uk.net

For help, advice or further information regarding Domestic Violence Against Women, contact Women's Aid at www.womensaid.org.uk or Refuge at www.refuge.org.uk or the Women & Equality Unit at www.womenandequalityunit.gov.uk/domestic_violence/index The Home Office (2003), *Male Victims of Domestic Violence.*

For help, advice or further information regarding *Domestic Violence Against Children*, contact the NSPCC at www.nspcc.org.uk or The Hideout: Domestic Violence Against Children and Young People at www.thehideout.org.uk or Women's Aid at www.womensaid.org.uk

For help, advice or further information regarding *Domestic Violence Against the Elderly*, contact Action on Elder Abuse (AEA) at www.elderabuse.org.uk or Women's Aid at www.womensaid.org.uk or Refuge at www.refuge.org.uk or the Women & Equality Unit at www.womenandequalityunit.gov.uk/domestic_violence/index

Information on *Rohypnol* researched from www.a1b2c3.com in November 2008 and updated February 2010.

Information on date rape drugs researched from www.talktofrank.com in January 2010.

Domestic Violence, Crime & Victims Act 2004.

Sexual Offences Act 2003.

'Kid Shield' have statistics on registered Paedophiles living in your area (UK) taken from annual MAPPA reports. If you want to read this or simply want advice on child safety from sexual predators, visit www.kidshield.co.uk

Tony Martin case study researched from various newspaper articles;
Audrey Gillan (April 2000), *"Life for farmer who shot burglar"*, 'The Guardian' newspaper.
Steven Morris (September 2003), *"Martin burglar back in custody"*, 'The Sun' newspaper.
Mike Jones (October 2001), *"Tony Martin sentence cut"*, 'The Sun' newspaper.
And various other related articles from BBC News, 2000 & 2003.

Kevin Jackson case study researched from www.forensic.gov.uk (2008).

Suzy Lamplugh case study researched from *"The search for Suzy"* article from BBC News on www.news.bbc.co.uk/1/hi/uk/551283 and various newspaper articles from the day.

Colour Sergeant Carl Tatton information researched from Olinka Koster (October 2007), *"'Incredible Hulk' Royal Marine lifts two-ton truck off drowning comrade during gun battle in Afghanistan"*, 'The Daily Mail' newspaper.

Liberal Democrat MP, Robert Brown (4th October 2009) statement in Scottish Parliament regarding *Domestic Violence* incidents increasing by double over last decade.

Lieutenant Colonel John Dean "Jeff" Cooper's colour code awareness system – developed for US Marines in the 1960's and still being used today by military personnel, law enforcement officials and close protection officers (not forgetting personal safety trainers and self defence instructors).